TROPICAL STYLE

Private Palm Beach

TROPICAL STYLE

Private Palm Beach

JENNIFER ASH

PHOTOGRAPHY BY ALEX MCLEAN

ABBEVILLE PRESS • PUBLISHERS
NEW YORK • LONDON

For Joe

Jacket front: Architect Maurice Fatio almost always created ornate entrances, as these elaborately carved front doors and arched ceilings attest.

Jacket back: Statuary graces the garden of Villa di Venezia. This palatial Mediterranean-style house, commissioned in 1930 by Harold Vanderbilt, now belongs to Melvin and Bren Simon.

Half-title page: Chameleons are a common sight on the island.

Frontispiece: This gazebo features a painting by William Benjamin that depicts how the view from the gazebo might have looked in the 1920s. See page 86.

Title page: Hedges such as these are ubiquitous in Palm Beach.

Editor: Jacqueline Decter
Designer: Adriane Stark
Production Editor: Sarah Key
Production Supervisor: Hope Koturo

Compilation, including selection of text and images, copyright © 1992 Abbeville Press, Inc.
Text copyright © 1992 Jennifer Ash

ISBN-10 1-55859-489-2
ISBN-13 978-1-55859-489-0

First edition
10 9 8 7 6 5 4

Photographs on pages 8–13 courtesy of
The Historical Society of Palm Beach County.
Photographs in the chapter "High-Style Villa" are reproduced with the permission of Ezra Stoller © Esto, all rights reserved (pages 40–41, 43–47) and C. J. Walker (page 42).

Library of Congress Cataloging-in-Publication Data
Ash, Jennifer.
    Private Palm Beach: tropical style/text by Jennifer Ash; photographs by Alex McLean.
        p. cm.
    Includes bibliographical references.
    ISBN 1-55859-269-5
        1-55859-489-2 (Tropical Style)
    1. Architecture, Tropical—Florida—Palm Beach. 2. Palm Beach (Fla.)—Buildings, structures, etc. I. McLean, Alex. II. Title.
    NA735.P35A84   1992
    728'.37'0975932—dc20   92-16008

For bulk and premium sales and for text adoption procedures, write to Customer Service Manager, Abbeville Press, 137 Varick Street, New York, NY 10013 or call 1-800-Artbook.

Author's Note

It's hard to believe that the first edition of this book was photographed and written before the advent of cell phones, the Internet, and spell check. In 1992, the chapters I wrote were double-spaced hardcopies, delivered via express post, and hand-raked for typos. In stark contrast to that slow process, I sent this author's note over the Internet to my editor with a thumb click. Palm Beach has kept in step with the times too. Just before the first issue came off the press, Donald Trump purchased Mar-a-Lago, an ocean-to-lake estate that remains one of Palm Beach's most storied mansions. Locals ridiculed the seven million dollar purchase price. Trump, they claimed, had finally made a bad deal. Thirteen years later, a vacant lakefront lot, less than eight hundred yards away from Trump's property and one-fourth the size, was purchased for over fifteen million and no one blinked.

This book captures a moment in time in Palm Beach and includes houses that are no longer standing and some owners who, sadly, are no longer living. When Dorothy Munn passed away, so did a unique way of life represented by her now-destroyed oceanfront home, Amado, with its white-jacketed butlers and discreet call bells hidden under the dining room table. The breezy pink Bermuda house built near the Munn property by Dorris Magowan is gone as well, but one can still imagine her handmade needlepoint rugs and simple rattan furniture arranged in cozy, informal groupings. Syms Murray, owner of the Buoyant Beach Cottage, has also passed away. Scavenger's Reward, the Vicarage, and the Grand Comfort houses have all changed ownership, and Crili has been traded for a new luxury boat. The Bohemian Cottage once owned by artist Nancy Jolly and the chapel on the lake that decorator Mimi McMakin calls home still stand, but as real estate on this tiny island becomes increasingly valuable, residents are pressured to make use of every square foot of property. Consequently, many old, charming, but high maintenance houses with rambling wooden porches and overgrown gardens are being torn down to make way for climate controlled places. These more functional homes boast artfully designed miniature green spaces but the basic vision remains the same; Palm Beach interiors continue to reflect the travels, imaginations, and whimsies of worldly individuals. These homes aren't copied from the pages of interior design magazines or European villas. They reflect a distinctive, subtropical Palm Beach lifestyle as illustrated by the home of Lilly Pulitzer Rousseau, where guests entertained under her glorious gazebo kick off even their treasured Manolo Blahniks at the door.

My husband and I are lucky enough to have our own little North End cottage. We have decorated it with a mishmash of castoffs found in nearby Dixie Highway shops. We like to think the sentimental decorating somehow preserves the way of life I knew growing up in Palm Beach. Our children ride bikes freely to friends' houses, drop fishing lines on the bike path, and carry their surfboards to Reef Road just as I did. Nighttime means cookouts, candlelight, jeans, and a door always ajar to admit friends who come and go. It's the kindheartedness of the people in Palm Beach that reminds me that whatever goes on in the rest of the world, this remains a gentle, tranquil place where consideration for your neighbors is as fundamental as the sunshine. The other day, while walking on the bike path, a man tipped his hat to me; I hope he has a grandson who is taking notes.

Jennifer Ash
Palm Beach, Florida
March, 2006

Acknowledgments

My sincere thanks to everyone who allowed me into their homes, offered friendly advice, and took an interest in this project, including Mr. and Mrs. Harry Loy Anderson, Aggie Attebury, Katy Basore, Mary Batsch, Mr. and Mrs. Joseph Bernstein, Reginald Boardman, Mary Bolton, Pat Booth, Nancy Brinker, Thomas Britt, Mr. and Mrs. Eugene Brown, Donald Bruce, Mr. and Mrs. William Buckley, Mr. and Mrs. Edwin Burke, Mr. and Mrs. Selig Burrows, Christina Orr-Cahall, Helen Cluett, Barbara Davidson, Mr. and Mrs. Alan Dayton, Mrs. Rodman de Heeren, Diane de la Bégassière, Dr. Nan Dennison, Margot de Peyster, Mr. and Mrs. Thomas Dittmer, Debbie Dolan, Mr. and Mrs. Russell Duncan, David Easton, Douglas Fairbanks, Jr., Eileen Fairchild, Mr. and Mrs. Alfonso Fanjul, Lillian Fernandez, Mr. and Mrs. Sam Fleming, Norma Foderer, Mr. and Mrs. Robert Fomon, Leta Foster, Mr. and Mrs. Robert Gardiner, Jenny Garrigues, Louis Gartner, Arij Gasiunasen, Letitia Gates, Mr. and Mrs. F. Warrington Gillet, Jr., Mr. and Mrs. Robert Gordon, Marisia Gordon-Smith, Mr. and Mrs. Kurt Goudy, James Griffen, Pamela Gross, Audrey Gruss, Mrs. Walter Gubelmann, C. Z. Guest, Mr. and Mrs. Christopher Hill, Page Hufty, Mr. and Mrs. Philip Hulitar, Geordi Humphries, Walter Irving, Nancy Jolly, David Kay, Robert Kirkland, Kirby Kooluris, Mr. and Mrs. Raymond Kravis, Mrs. Joseph Lauder, Mr. and Mrs. Tom Leddy, Norris McFarlane, Carol Mack, Sondra and David S. Mack, Mimi McMakin, Mrs. Robert Magowan, Jean Mahoney, Mr. and Mrs. Terrence Mahoney, Mrs. Jack Massey, Mr. and Mrs. Frederick Melhado, Carola Mendel, Dina Merrill, Mrs. Charles Munn, Sims Murray, Douglas Mutch, Mr. and Mrs. S. I. Newhouse, Dr. Charles Nichols, Mr. and Mrs. William Pannill, Mr. and Mrs. Andreall Pearson, Mr. and Mrs. John Pickett, Mr. and Mrs. John Pomerantz, James Ponce, Paul Prosperi, Arlett Rigby, John Romande, Lilly Rousseau, Eleanor Rudick, Mr. and Mrs. Allan Scherer, Mr. and Mrs. Kim Seargent, Eve Siegal, Mr. and Mrs. Mel Simon, Scott Snyder, Kathy Tankoos, Donald Trump, Alexandra Vassilopoulos, David Veselsky, Jane Volk, Mr. and Mrs. Peter Warburton, Peter Werner, Leslie Clayton-White, Tom Wicky, Charles Wieland, Mr. and Mrs. Don Wright, Stephanie Wrightsman, and Jane Ylvisaker, as well as those who prefer to remain unmentioned. I would like to express appreciation to my friend Susan Magrino, who originally encouraged me to pursue this idea.

This book owes everything to the expert and affable guidance received from everyone at Abbeville Press. Special thanks to Alan Mirken, who has been enthusiastic about this project from the outset, and to Mark Magowan for his unerring taste. As a longtime visitor to Palm Beach, his comments were especially sensitive and valuable. I am particularly thankful to my editor, Jackie Decter, whose deft command of the English language, sure sense of proportion, and ever-present sense of humor made every stage of this book a true delight. It was also a joy to work with publicity director Rozelle Shaw. Alex McLean's discerning eye, unflappability, and diligence turned long days of photographing into a pleasure, and Adriane Stark's inspired design enhanced the liveliness of his photographs.

I am greatly indebted to those who have already written about Palm Beach, including Donald Curl, Barbara Hoffstot, Judge James Knott, and all of the journalists who have covered the town and whose books and articles I drew upon freely. I immensely appreciated those who granted interviews enabling this book to contain personal anecdotes and histories never before written. A heartfelt thanks to Agnes and Clarke Ash, who patiently and generously shared their priceless knowledge about the town and its people.

Most importantly, I thank my husband, Joe Rudick, who was always first to advise on pictures and text, and who was unfailingly supportive of an unpredictable schedule and my constant, often lengthy visits to Palm Beach, a remarkable island that I will always feel privileged to consider home. – Jennifer Ash

Contents

Introduction

One question about Palm Beach has intrigued novelists, historians, and the media for decades: "What lies behind the hedges?" Hedges are such a basic feature of the island's landscape that a local law regulates their trimming and protects them from destruction. If an endowment for hedges could be established, no other institution in town would be more heavily funded.

This foliage fanaticism is not botanical in origin. Rather, it stems from a fierce devotion to privacy that has been passed down from generation to generation. Ever since the height of walls was restricted by the town code, hedges have been serving as live barricades protecting the super rich from public scrutiny. These leafy curtains allow them to indulge impulse more freely.

The people who live behind the hedges are frequently eccentric, unfailingly philanthropic, and determined to do as they please. Their wondrous residential fantasies, inspired by the natural beauty of this subtropical barrier island only fourteen miles long and no more than half a mile wide, are testimony to what can be achieved when imagination, rather than money, is the only limitation.

Lake Worth, the part of the Intracoastal Waterway that separates this island from West Palm Beach on the mainland,

Will Lanehart's house

was named for Colonel William Jenkins Worth, who was in command of federal troops in the latter part of the Seminole Indian War. Worth was later second-in-command of U.S. forces in the Mexican War, and Fort Worth, Texas, is also named for him.

Palm Beach's first nonmilitary settlers arrived in 1873, joining a Civil War draft dodger who had moved to the island in 1862. By 1877 there were nineteen families. One of the very first houses was built entirely of flotsam and jetsam washed to shore by the Atlantic Ocean. It was believed to belong to Will Lanehart, a cousin of Ben Lainhart (*sic*), whose descendants still reside in the area. At this time Palm Beach was called the Lake Worth Cottage Colony. It was landscaped with palm trees quite by accident in 1878, when the *Providencia*, a small Spanish brigantine carrying a cargo of twenty thousand coconuts, was wrecked offshore. Settlers planted the coconuts, thereby giving birth to the island's tropical appeal.

Around the mid-1880s Henry Morrison Flagler, a Standard Oil partner and Florida real estate developer, brought his railroads to St. Augustine, where he had built the Ponce de Leon Hotel. It marked the Florida resort frontier until Flagler visited Palm Beach and became so enchanted by it that in 1893 he erected the Royal Poinciana Hotel on the island and then extended the Florida East Coast Railroad to Lake Worth.

With the Ponce de Leon Hotel, which was designed by John M. Carrère and Thomas Hastings, two young apprentices at the New York firm, McKim, Mead and White, Flagler introduced Mediterranean architecture to Florida. When Flagler moved on to Palm Beach, however, he opted for clapboard and shingle structures adapted from the seaside styles popular in Bar Harbor and Southampton, and he gave the job to another young architect, Theodore Blake. As Florida historians point out, Flagler built at his leisure in St. Augustine, whereas he was creating Palm Beach during boom times. Wooden structures, even when they rose to six stories, could be built in a few months; stone archways and stucco walls took longer. The Royal Poinciana Hotel was painted a sunny yellow that came to be known as Flagler yellow. The furnishings were white wicker with green fabrics, a combination found in many Palm Beach houses to this day.

Flagler's next project was Palm Beach's first mansion, a columned Greek Revival house called Whitehall, which he presented to his third wife, Mary Lily Kenan, as a wedding gift in 1901. Carrère & Hastings, who had by then gained a reputation as architects to the wealthy, finished the mansion, which is now a museum, for just under $2.5 million. At the

The Royal Poinciana Hotel

time, its immense stucco outline stood in jarring contrast to the wooden frame houses of the cottage colony.

Meanwhile, in 1898 Colonel Edward Bradley opened the Beach Club, a gambling casino that was the first in the nation to allow ladies at the gaming tables. It was a sprawling wooden structure in the expedient architectural style of the day. Bradley circumvented Florida's state ban on gambling simply by not allowing any full-time state residents to become members of his club. Thousands of dollars, a few yachts, and many shares of stock changed hands nightly at the casino. It was strictly black tie after six o'clock in the evening; thus Palm Beach's penchant for formal dress was indelibly inked into the season's schedule. One afternoon, automobile magnate Walter Chrysler was playing roulette and forgot the time. Bradley asked him to go home and change into proper evening attire. Chrysler refused on the grounds that he was down $20,000. Bradley offered to flip a coin, double or nothing. The colonel made the toss, then, without looking at the coin, put it away, saying, "You win, go home and get dressed." Bradley had instinctive style and his customers had no option but to follow his lead.

Bradley endeared himself to his customers even after his death. In his will, he asked that the casino be torn down so that unscrupulous gamblers couldn't move in after him. He bequeathed the property to the town on the condition that it become a public park, and in the event that the town did not remove the buildings, the property was to be turned over to the Catholic Church.

In 1895 Flagler built the Palm Beach Inn to handle the overflow from the Royal Poinciana. It opened in 1896 and proved to be so popular that it was enlarged three times by 1901, when it was renamed the Breakers. In 1903 the Breakers burned down; a new one opened its doors in 1904, but it, too, succumbed to flames in 1925. Dr. William Rand Kenan, Jr., who had taken over the Flagler System after Henry Flagler's death in 1913, built the present Breakers in 1926 in less than

Bradley's Beach Club

a year. The Royal Poinciana was eventually torn down in the early thirties.

Vacationers stayed at the Breakers Hotel, fell in love with the island, and made plans to build equally lavish homes. With the success of the Breakers, Palm Beach became securely established as a wealthy winter resort town.

In 1918 two flamboyant friends—Paris Singer, heir to the sewing-machine fortune, and architect Addison Mizner—visited Palm Beach and found it somewhat too sleepy for their liking. Singer was a world traveler and had had a turbulent affair

with dancer Isadora Duncan. Mizner was born in 1872 in Benicia on the north side of San Francisco Bay. In 1889 his father was appointed United States envoy-minister to five Central American countries and the family moved to Guatemala, where Addison was exposed to sixteenth- and seventeenth-century Spanish colonial architecture. After attending Spain's University of Salamanca, Mizner served a three-year apprenticeship under San Francisco architect Willis Polk. This was his only formal architecture training. In 1904 Mizner moved to New York, where he was provided with introductions into swank social circles and began selling his new friends objets d'art he had collected on his travels throughout China, Central America, Spain, Italy, and the South Pacific. Soon he began receiving architecture commissions, including several cast off by Stanford White, and built many houses on Long Island, some in the Mediterranean style. But after being mugged by three hitchhikers whom he had picked up on his way home from a party, Mizner wanted to leave New York and Singer convinced him to come to Palm Beach to convalesce. With Singer's money, Mizner's expertise, and plenty of time on their hands, the two men set about redesigning the face of Palm Beach.

Together they gave the hotel community a boost by building

Mediterranean-style shops and clubs, and they gave their friends the confidence to have fun with their money by building equally lavish mansions in the same style. Mizner's first such commission came from Eva Stotesbury, whose husband, Edward T., was a senior partner in the Morgan Company. Eva, who was sometimes thought of as a caricature of the social dowager, is remembered for her witty retorts. A woman who was aghast at the way Mrs. Stotesbury spent money once said to her, "Pearls during the daytime?" Without missing a beat Mrs. Stotesbury replied, "Yes my dear. I used to feel the same way. But that was before I had pearls." For her, Mizner designed and built El Mirasol. Its massive stone and tile gateway still stands off North County Road, but the forty-acre estate has since been subdivided and there remains only a street named in its honor.

Mizner continued to build, sometimes with Singer's financing, sometimes on commission. The client would leave in the spring, pressing a check into Mizner's hand, and return the next season to find his Palm Beach dream house a reality, resplendent with stucco walls, spiral staircases, soaring beamed ceilings, pecky cypress paneling, loggias, wide balconies, and cloistered walkways. The wood Mizner used was aged in his workrooms in West Palm Beach, where new lumber was beaten with chains and paint was applied and then partially removed to give the wood a rubbed, worn look. When worm holes were needed, the wood was peppered with buckshot. Mizner spent

Addison Mizner

much of the year traveling in Europe, chiefly in Spain, where he bought entire rooms from villas and monasteries, sometimes not bothering to ask if he was dealing with the rightful owner.

In 1925, at the height of the Florida building boom, Mizner began developing Boca Raton, south of Palm Beach, and Paris Singer launched the development of Singer Island to the north. But almost immediately the boom collapsed and the hurricanes of 1926 and 1928 further dampened the ardor for Florida real estate. The stock market crash of 1929 finished off all hope of Mizner's revival. By the early thirties Mizner's health was failing, but those friends who had managed to survive the Depression rallied to support him financially. He died of a heart attack on November 5, 1933. His high-living, high-rolling brother Wilson amused him right up to the end. When the architect was on his deathbed, Wilson sent him a telegram from Hollywood, where he was writing a screenplay. "Stop dying. Am trying to write a comedy." The response came back: "Am going to get well. The comedy goes on."

When renowned Viennese architect and designer Joseph Urban came to the United States during World War I, he first found work in Hollywood and on Broadway. Having designed sets for the Metropolitan Opera and for Florenz Ziegfeld's famous Follies, he was a natural choice to redesign two Palm Beach night clubs, the Club de Montmartre in 1925 and the Oasis Club in 1927. Between these projects he designed the private Bath and Tennis Club, which is reminiscent of the

Lido, as well as the Paramount Theater and its adjoining Sunrise shops. E. F. Hutton and Anthony Drexel Biddle supplied the capital for the project. The theater, now a landmark building divided into office space, was noted for its wavelike cypress ceiling and a mural two stories high depicting underwater creatures. Urban's greatest vote of confidence, however, came when Marjorie Merriweather Post—at the time married to E. F. Hutton—asked him to work on Mar-a-Lago, an estate set on eighteen acres stretching from ocean to lake. Built between 1923 and 1927, the mansion boasts perhaps the most dramatic outdoor entertaining space in all of Palm Beach—a cloistered courtyard featuring a pebble-design walkway inspired by the Alhambra in Spain. The living room's gilded ceiling was inspired by the Galleria Dell'Accademia's Thousand Wing ceiling in Venice.

El Mirasol, designed by Addison Mizner

Before the Huttons met Urban, another prominent Palm Beach architect, Marion Sims Wyeth, who had built the couple's Golfview Road house, had begun to design Mar-a-Lago. Wyeth, whose grandfather J. Marion Sims founded New York's Women's Hospital, and whose father, John Wyeth, founded New York's Polyclinic Hospital, moved to Palm Beach in 1919, only two years after Addison Mizner, leaving his job at Carrère & Hastings. Although Mizner offered him a position, Wyeth began his own company, Wyeth and King, with business partner Rhinelander King. Wyeth's work was less dramatic than Mizner's and his plans were meticulously thought out, perhaps as a result of his training at the Ecole des Beaux-Arts in Paris. There he was awarded the Prix Jean LeClerc in 1913 and the Deuxième Prix Rougevin in 1914, and he became the first Palm Beach architect to be elected a fellow of the American Institute of Architects.

Paris-educated Wyeth and Maurice Fatio, a dashing Swiss architect, became good friends when Fatio moved to Palm Beach in 1925. Fatio graduated from the Polytechnical School at the University of Zurich and studied under Swiss architect Karl Moser. In Palm Beach he began designing harmonious Mediterranean-style houses and eventually branched out into everything from Georgian to contemporary.

Howard Major, who also came to Palm Beach in 1925, with a degree from Pratt Institute, was a chief proponent of Georgian style, especially as it had been adapted in the British West Indies. By the end of the thirties Major's less pretentious and adorned forms became the favored style in Palm Beach.

John Volk, a Columbia graduate, came to the island in 1926 and became one of Palm Beach's most prolific architects, obtaining over one thousand commissions. He proved he could design in almost any style, from Colonial (such as his own house, White Gables) and Mediterranean (his buildings on

Worth Avenue) to Regency (the Poinciana Playhouse) and modern (including a house called La Ronda on North Lake Drive). For one of his most eccentric clients, Lily Fuller, Volk built a house with a resplendent Portuguese tile roof. Now owned by Mr. and Mrs. Robert Fomon, it is endearingly called the Buddha House by locals. When Lily wanted a smaller house, she commissioned Volk to build a Samoan-looking structure complete with a goldfish pond; it is now owned by Mrs. Walter Gubelmann, whose sense of style and wit are strong enough to carry off the house.

Whatever idiosyncratic whims architects have catered to over the years, they must take the island's subtropical setting into consideration. Kitchens are placed in the northwest part of houses so that prevailing southeast winds don't reveal what's being cooked to the rest of the house. Ceilings are high and peppered with fans. Palm Beach architect Jeff Smith continues to use design elements that have been employed since the town's inception. "We, like Mizner, use a lot of loggias as a way not only to connect rooms but also to allow you to sit outside when it is raining and the temperature is still nice." Some wooden houses are raised slightly off the ground so that winds can sweep above and below the structure. An example is the "stick" house at the corner of Seabreeze and Cocoanut Row, painted an intense orange at the suggestion of the

The Oasis Club, designed by Joseph Urban

owner's friend, the late designer Isabelle O'Neill.

Because of the intensity and profusion of light, colors are used in abundance. Stephanie Wrightsman, who lives in a pale brick house on the island's north end, is constantly recoloring her interiors. At the time this book was written the living room was hydrangea orange, the staircase Flagler yellow, and a bathroom orchid violet; these colors suit the island perfectly.

Patios and outdoor living space are prized, especially if they are surrounded by hedges and other foliage. Hedges soar thirty feet beside the modest tennis house that gardening author C. Z. Guest retained as her tropical hideaway when the Guest estate, Villa Artemis, was sold after the death of Mrs. Frederick Churchill Guest. Hedges fifty feet high shielded Charles Wrightsman's famous oceanfront villa, but the new owner demolished the Fatio-designed house hours before the Landmarks Commission could build legal barricades strong enough to stop the bulldozers.

Sadly, Palm Beach has lost some of its most significant residences. However, many—big and small—remain, and our camera has penetrated the hedges behind which they normally hide. A number of the houses on these pages have never before been photographed for publication. Permission to do so was motivated by the need to document a life-style and craftsmanship that are unique to this enchanting island.

JUNGLE PARADISE

When Lilly Pulitzer Rousseau first went into business selling fruit from her husband's groves in the posh Via Parigi, she usurped a corner of her own fruit stand and began selling shifts made from  bright Key West fabrics. Palm Beachers immediately abandoned their lifelong pledges to white pants and seersucker shirts in favor of these new, upbeat resort uniforms in hot pink, brilliant yellow, and pea- pod green. The "Lilly" dress was to Palm Beach what long shorts were to Bermuda. Fashionable women from Martha's Vineyard, Massachusetts, to Sea Island, Georgia, wore Lilly's slender, lace-trimmed dresses throughout the 1960s and 1970s. During the 1980s, when the dresses were not being produced, they became the most treasured finds at Palm Beach Day School's spring rummage sale. Now new designs are sold in resort towns across the country.

Lilly set another trend in Palm Beach. For the women who admired her—and all of them did—hard work became fashionable and indolence a sign of limited imagination. Many launched careers, opening shops, real estate offices, and travel agencies in town. In the 1960s Lilly's fast-expanding business—she owned stores nationwide and a factory in Miami—left her no time to fuss over a formal household. In those days she lived in a turn-of-the-century clapboard house, now owned by Harry Loy and Inger Anderson, which she decorated with her near-neon fabrics. It was filled with natural wicker, authentic Tiffany chandeliers, French porcelain stoves, and a pool table. At home Lilly always went barefoot, even at her parties. For a time, Palm Beach's social epicenter was Lilly's enormous kitchen, where everyone watched her cook.

Now she lives about a mile to the south of her first lakeside house in a residence she has designed as a jungle preserve. With the exception of a few pot holders and a collage in her bedroom, there is little evidence of her former business in her current house. "I didn't want to use those fabrics here, I lived with them for years," she says. Thankfully, little else has changed. Lilly still goes barefoot, and dinner, usually served in an enormous slat house, is always casual. Anyone with a robust appetite is welcome.

Lilly designed the house in 1984, carefully tailoring the plans at every step to take full advantage of her beloved jungle. When it was finally time to execute the plans, she realized that the lusher part of the property was on the north side and that the entire house would have to be flipped around so the loggia would face that way. "That was the final straw for the architect," she recalls with a laugh. Her laugh, as everyone in Palm Beach knows, wins Lilly absolution for the most capricious changes of direction.

Preceding pages
Left: Set in a veritable jungle, the house provides a wonderful sense of escape from the manicured community in which it stands. Right: Photographs of Lilly's children growing up in Palm Beach cover every inch of her office walls. The picture on the left is of Lilly herself in one of her famous dresses.

Left: A wooden carving of an angel was transformed into a lamp and presides over a collection of photographs of family and friends in the living room. Right: The living room is decorated in an uncommon mixture of colorful stripes, floral patterns, paisleys, and batiks concocted by Lilly Pulitzer Rousseau. The large, delicately carved and swagged wood and iron chandelier was purchased in West Palm Beach from Peter Werner.

The jungle motif is carried
out throughout the house.
This decorative elephant
sits beneath a mirror that
reflects the exotic fabrics
used in the living room.

Entering the house is like stepping into the pages of the *Jungle Book*. It is a welcome contradiction to the carefully manicured island on which it stands. "I don't like going beyond, or leaving, the jungle," says Lilly, who spends nearly twelve months a year in Palm Beach. From every undraped window there are views of banana, citrus, and palm trees. "I'm not one for curtains, I like to see a lot of the outdoors," she says.

The layout of the main house is simple. The huge living room, with its thirty-foot-high peaked ceiling, has floor-to-ceiling windows on the east and south walls. This room opens onto a loggia, which in turn looks onto the pool. A gallery leading from the loggia to the kitchen serves as the dining room, where a French baker's rack is used to store pottery, and a large antique French bird cage is alive with parakeets and their playmates—big, stuffed Lilly-fabric parrots. The kitchen is always busy, as Lilly's casual house encourages constant traffic.

Behind the slat house, paths through the jungle lead to a number of unexpected surprises, from Jacuzzis and barbecue areas to wish-fulfilling play areas for children. Tucked behind a grove of banana trees is a two-story vine-covered guest house.

All of these additional attractions accommodate nine grandchildren, visiting friends, numerous cats, and a pit bull. "Everyone should live in harmony," says Lilly, whose sense of ease in her unconventional house, as in all things, brings out the best in everyone. Even the pit bull is all bark.

The dining room is in the gallery leading from the loggia to the kitchen. Piñatas in the shape of chickens swathed in tulle and faux pearls make perfect centerpieces for an Easter-weekend bridal dinner.

The slat house, reminiscent of those built for Palm Beach houses in the 1920s, is used for entertaining rather than for housing plants. The huge picnic tables are covered with brightly printed Key West fabric, once used for Lilly's dress designs. Chandeliers made of seashells are from Key West's Shell City. In the distance the pool can be seen.

The pool, one of the largest in Palm Beach, serves the Rousseau family all year round. Unlike most of the island's residents, the Rousseaus do not leave their beloved island, even in the sweltering heat of summer.

PALM BEACH CLASSIC

*N*ewcomers to Palm Beach seek access to the "inner circle." Some are motivated by innocent curiosity; others want to position themselves socially. Before World War II, and until about 1975, the  stratifications were clearly marked but today Palm Beach has a multitude of social circles, all linked and overlapping like the Olympic symbol. There are, however, a few remaining traces of the era when the social order was as well defined as the charts in Burke's Peerage. The most recognizable but also the most privately held piece of property is Amado, the mansion built in 1919 by Addison Mizner for Charles Munn, his first wife, Mary Drexel Paul, and their four children. Not long afterward, Mary and Charles divorced. Mary Munn married a Frenchman and spent the rest of her life in Paris. Charles, who remained unwed for many years, became the great host of Palm Beach. He was so identified with the island that all his friends knew him as "Mr. Palm Beach." With his wit and charming manners, the tall, dark, and handsome Charles made many friends both here and

**Preceding pages
Left: A butler's jacket
hangs on the screen that
conceals the door to the
kitchen from the dining
room. Right: Amado was
built in 1919 by Mizner for
Charles Munn, Jr. The
original approach to the
house was from this side
until a road separating the
house from the ocean was
washed away.**

**Left: Louis XV open-arm
chairs decorate the drawing
room, where a large
Oriental-style mirrored
screen conceals a movie
projector used by the
Munns during film parties.
Right: A Vargueno desk,
procured by Addison Mizner
for Charles Munn, is topped
with a leather letter box
and an oil painting by
Prince Fran Windwisch-
Graetz.**

abroad. There were few families more closely associated with Palm Beach's original social set than the Munns.

An inventor of sorts, Charles earned his first fortune by creating a mechanical mail-sorting machine. Later the entrepreneur increased his fortune on racetrack machinery, buying the rights to a mechanical rabbit he saw in action at a Miami dog track in the 1920s. Munn introduced the system to several tracks in England and it proved to be a great success. He and friends Robert Grant, a partner in the brokerage firm of Lee Higginson Co., and John C. King of Palm Beach began raising money to market it throughout England. Eventually they bought about five British tracks.

At these and other racetracks, Munn operated a triangle odds machine called a totalisator, which he discovered in Australia. It was the first machine of its kind in America when Charles leased it to Joseph Widener for his Hialeah track, where it became known as a parimutuel machine.

With his fortune in place, Charles Munn, along with his brothers, Gurnee and Ector, were at the forefront of Palm Beach's throbbing social scene. Like his friend the Duke of Windsor, Charles was a distinguished dresser, often credited with popularizing the casual resort look indigenous to Palm Beach. He initiated the tradition of a Christmas card listing his friends and their private phone numbers. The list defined Palm Beach's inner circle. The tradition is continued to this day by another Palm Beach family.

Amado, one of the island's original mansions, is testimony to the town's heyday, from the 1920s to the late 1970s. It is the only house designed by society architect Addison Mizner that remains in the possession of the family for whom it was built.

To enter Amado is to step back in time. Amazingly, the house and its grounds remain unchanged; the only exception is the disappearance of an access road, destroyed during a hurricane in 1928, that separated the house from the ocean. At the time Charlie Munn gladly noted, "Now I have oceanfront property."

A generous, deep green lawn of Bermuda grass dotted with slender coconut palms now stretches from the house to the ocean. Shielding the estate from North County Road are a pool, a large, informal rose garden, vegetable gardens, fruit trees, a caretaker's cottage, and low, leafy palm trees.

Architect Addison Mizner insisted on furnishing the public rooms of the houses he built but left the decor of the private rooms up to the owners. "I don't care what they do in their bedroom," he was often quoted as saying. The Mediterranean style favored by the architect could be austere, so he filled his houses with rich-looking pieces legally scavenged from crumbling churches and monasteries in Europe. As his building business boomed, Mizner opened a factory called Mizner Industry in West Palm Beach, where he replicated the furniture to fill his increasing orders. Seventeenth-century Spanish furniture was reproduced down to the worm holes, which were achieved with ice picks and buckshot. Wood was scraped with broken bottles to give it a worn look. Blacksmiths made wrought-iron lighting fixtures and gates. The entire dining room at Amado remains as Mizner furnished it in the 1920s. But the only other original Mizner furnishings left in the house are a few pieces in the library and the Spanish leather chairs in the hall.

In 1954 Charles got married again—this time to one of America's most well-known socialites, Dorothy Spreckels, the daughter of Adolph Spreckels, the San Francisco sugar magnate, and his wife, Alma. Dorothy had previously been married to a Frenchman, Jean Dupuy, owner of *Le Petit Parisian*, a Paris newspaper.

When Dorothy (who was very keen on decorating houses) married Charles Munn, she found that because Mr. Munn had considered Amado a beach house to visit during the winter months with his first wife and four children, the interiors of the house lacked the beauty of its exterior.

The first thing she did was install a parquet floor over the simulated stone in the entrance hall, which later became the scene of many dinner dances and movie parties. First-run movies would be shown on a screen that rolled down from a ceiling beam in the spacious hall. The projection room was hidden behind a mirrored screen in the adjoining drawing room. Next Dorothy built a pool and pool house in the west flower garden. Finally, she turned her attention to redecorating the

Sketches from the Lido and photographs of family and friends, including David Niven and the Duke of Westminster, collected over a lifetime, give the bar a festive feeling.

The "blue" guest room,
overlooking the ocean, was
furnished by Dorothy Munn
in the 1950s when she
married Charles Munn.

Right: Jean de Botton's
painting of Dorothy Munn's
Paris apartment hangs in
the library, where Dorothy
Munn, a champion bridge
player, plays almost daily.
Regency chairs and end
tables sit on a 1725 Turkish
Oushaka rug. Fortuny
draperies frame the windows.

entire third floor, which in 1954 looked more like a series of hotel rooms than the rooms of a private residence. To quote Mrs. Munn, "It was fun to do because it was structurally well thought out with a walk-in closet in each bedroom and a window in each bathroom."

Dorothy and Charles Munn were one of international society's most glamorous couples. During the season, they entertained frequently and the house overflowed with guests, some of whom stayed as long as a month.

Of the four Munn children, the eldest, Pauline Munn Doyle, died in 1937 of septicemia and Charles Munn, Jr., died in 1958 of Lou Gehrig's disease. The two surviving children are Mary, who is married to Eric, the Earl of Bessborough, son of the former Governor General of Canada, and Frances, whose first husband was George F. Baker II of Citibank. She is presently Mrs. Bezencenet and lives in Paris. Both daughters visit Amado each year.

Charlotte, the Bessboroughs's only child, is married to Yanni Petsupoulis and lives in London. There are three Baker children, two of whom—Anthony and Pauline (Mrs. Dixon Boardman)— live in Palm Beach and have beautiful houses of their own. George Baker III lives in New York City. Charles Munn, Jr.'s one son, Charles A. Munn III, is an authority on parrots, particularly the hyacinth macaw, and is associated with the New York Zoological Society.

There are three Mrs. Munns presently living in Palm Beach: Virginia, the wife of Ector Munn, who celebrated his 100th birthday in April 1991; Brigitte, the widow of Charles Munn's nephew, Gurnee Munn, Jr.; and, of course, Dorothy Munn. A

widow since 1981, Dorothy is no longer in good health, but continues to live at the estate, seeing old friends and playing bridge and backgammon. She keeps Amado fully staffed, just as it was in the old days, when house guests streamed in and out of every room.

The dining room remains just as architect Addison Mizner designed it, complete with a table he procured for Charles Munn in Europe.

The foyer, called the Great Hall by Palm Beachers, is decorated with tapestries and roses from Dorothy Munn's garden. This space was often used as an auxiliary dining room and as a dance floor. Mizner created the dramatic Moorish-style stairway.

ISLAND
RETREAT

ay off Palm Beach's beaten paths, down a road marked by two tall, eagle-topped posts, is a posh finger of land called Everglades Island. It was once known as Cabbage Island, for a lone cabbage palm that stood on its southernmost tip, and is one of many sandbars that follow the shorelines of Lake Worth. Most of these sandbars have been designated bird sanctuaries, making the only two that are inhabited, Everglades Island and Tarpon Island, particularly exclusive. In 1938 the Phipps family's Bessemer Properties, Inc., began developing Everglades Island, dredging soil from the bottom of the surrounding lake to lengthen the road leading to the island, where the company planned to build a retaining wall and create sixty lots, each with waterfront footage. The project had to be put

Preceding pages
Left: The house is situated
on an island's island, the
only one of its kind in Palm
Beach. It sits in a small
lagoon peppered with
uninhabited islands that are
now bird sanctuaries.
Right: French doors open
onto a screened porch that
has access to a stairway
leading to the swimming
pool terrace on the east side
of the house.

Above: A little wooden
bridge leads to the only
house in Palm Beach on a
private island, perhaps the
town's best-kept secret.

Left: Porches, balconies,
and Bermuda-style
pediments were added to
redesign the original boxy
shape of the house. The
entire exterior was glazed a
warm antique salmon color
to blend with a new terra-
cotta roof.

on hold during World War II, but it recommenced in 1946. During this second stage, the island road was extended to the much smaller freckle of land called Tarpon Island, which the company planned to develop into a single residential lot. The plot was sold to Wiley Reynolds for $12,000, about a hundredth of what it is worth today, as it remains the only privately owned island in Palm Beach. The three-acre island has a remote, almost isolated feeling. In reality, however, it is only yards away from the highly civilized Colony Hotel and Worth Avenue. Clients of designer David Anthony Easton fell in love with the property's envelope of greenery, which makes the house invisible until you have crossed the tiny wooden bridge leading to it. They were also attracted to the view of the Intracoastal Waterway and of its many small, uninhabited islands.

When the couple bought the house it was a rather nondescript boxy structure. They called upon Easton to restyle it for them. "The plan was there, we just wanted David to make the house a little more gracious," says the wife. Easton had already designed a number of residences for these clients. He gave their Chicago apartment a formal, high-style interior with ebony floors and white walls. In contrast, he decorated their Lake Forest house in a traditional, cordial English style and filled their Aspen ski retreat with earth-tone fabrics and contemporary American art.

Easton's first order of business in redesigning the Tarpon Island house was to alter its structure and maximize the number of water views. "The inside of the house was a warren of rooms, very additive and cluttered," Easton recalls. He cut an entry hall straight through the house from north to south. At the southern end of the hall he installed French doors, through which the lake can be seen. In the living room he framed the French stone mantel on the northern wall with large mirrors to reflect the lake view visible through the floor-to-ceiling bay windows on the southern wall. These windows are actually glass doors that can slide into the walls, turning the living room and its new south terrace into an indoor-outdoor space.

Left: White cabinets, a terra-cotta floor, and a country table set in a large bay window make the kitchen an inviting room.

The dining room and kitchen overlook an outdoor dining terrace that also faces Lake Worth. Likewise, large sliding windows with a view of the Intracoastal were installed in the master bedroom and bath.

Since the Tarpon Island house is a vacation home, Easton designed spaces for relaxing and unwinding. "I attempted to create a much simpler house than most of the houses I have seen in Palm Beach. I chose not to use a lot of expensive furniture." Instead, he opted for English, Portuguese, and French Provincial furniture with fabrics in natural and woven textures, and marvelous French printed cottons for the upholstery in the living room and the walls in the dining room. Sisal carpets are used in many of the rooms, and there are area rugs throughout the interiors. The easygoing tone is established in the living room, where a blue, cream, rose, and salmon pink cotton area rug covers a wall-to-wall sisal carpet. The area rug's warm rose tones are picked up in the upholstery and the curtains, and complement soft salmon-colored walls. Off the living room are two porches, each furnished with casual-looking rattan furniture and French outdoor furniture.

Below: In the living room the wall-to-wall sisal carpet is detailed with a blue, cream, and salmon pink cotton area rug. The furniture is covered in a French printed cotton from Brunschwig & Fils. A round English Regency table stands in the middle of the room. Mirrored screens, designed by David Easton's firm, are placed on either side of the north wall to reflect the view of the Intracoastal to the south.

Local fossil stone covers the floor of the east porch, where a set of Bielecky rattan furniture and a pair of Isle of Orkney chairs are grouped around a painted coffee table. The beamed ceiling and wooden paddle fans contribute to the sense of indoor-outdoor space that is so characteristic of houses in a subtropical climate. After years of facing the Intracoastal, the patina on the Italian bull's-eye mirror has flaked, softening the effect of the porch and the furniture.

Left: The master bedroom was designed around an antique needlepoint rug in soft salmon colors. The bed faces French doors that lead to a screened, covered porch.

Right: In the dining room the wall fabric, a French printed cotton in an Indian tree-of-life pattern, is the backdrop for a large French Provincial table and painted Portuguese chairs. The combination gives the room an islandy feel.

For the exterior Easton decided upon a Bermuda-style feeling. He glazed the entire facade an antique salmon color, painted the woodwork a fresh, creamy white, and added Bermuda-style pediments, a new terra-cotta roof, and deep green shutters. He also added two-story porches to the facades and terraces over-looking the pool. "Weather permitting, we were always on the porches," says the wife. Off the second-story rooms, he increased the number of balconies, all of which are accessible through French doors. "I think the house has a very islandy look," says Easton. The tropical style is validated when all of the doors are open and breezes come in off the water, filling this island retreat with the crisp, salty smell of sea air.

HIGH-STYLE VILLA

*T*he stark white house that soars gracefully above its lakefront neighbors is Palm Beach's first celebrated modern residence. Designed by architect  Richard Meier, it is a study in abstraction, of the way volume and light create and shape space. Like many contemporary architects, Meier has been influenced by the early masters of the Modern movement: Le Corbusier, Alvar Aalto, and Walter Gropius. His work is involved with the relationships between planar and linear elements, between that which is solid and that which is void. As in this house, he sometimes limits his material selection to white porcelain-steel panels and glass blocks, thus focusing attention on the architectural concerns of creating space.

Meier, the youngest recipient of the coveted Pritzker Prize for Architecture,

has designed many private residences throughout the country, but this house was his first commission in Florida. His most notable works include the High Museum of Art in Atlanta, the Museum for Decorative Arts in Frankfurt, the Canal+ Television Headquarters in Paris, and the Getty Center in Los Angeles, a campuslike grouping of buildings located on a 110-acre site in the foothills of the Santa Monica Mountains.

His Palm Beach house is the island's most sophisticated example of the time-honored idea of grand yet gracious space. Although the design is atypical of the architecture along the Lake Worth coastline, it refers to themes used in early European villas and reestablished in architect Addison Mizner's Palm Beach mansions of the 1920s.

"It is really two houses that work together or can be shut off from one another," says Meier, who, like Mizner, placed guest rooms on the opposite side of the house from the master suite and separated private rooms from public rooms.

The architect's first step was a careful inspection of the site. He had to work around the lot's narrow shape while emphasizing its spectacular water views to the west. "The house has no side, it has a front and a back," he says. To the north and south he planted ficus hedges that eclipse views of neighboring houses. "It was nice to plant the hedges because everything grew so well in the subtropical climate," says Meier, who had the opportunity to watch the hedges develop over the two-and-a-half years it took him to complete his meticulous design. Today, almost twenty years later, the hedges are the most impressive foliage along the local bicycle path; their sides are neatly trimmed

Below: This stairway leads to an upstairs study that overlooks the lake. The glass block allows light to penetrate the interior walls.

Preceding pages
Left: Square-shaped elements, such as these guest-suite windows and their reflection in the pool, are a key feature of Richard Meier's design.
Right: The house is essentially two separate structures. The guest wing is to the left, and the public rooms and master suite are to the right.

Right: In the entranceway, the door on the right leads to the public rooms. The one straight ahead opens onto the pool. The guest wing, to the left, is connected to the rest of the house by two open walkways.

but the tops have been left to grow even taller than hedges planted decades before.

Parallel to the lake Meier planned somewhat lower hedges so that the owners could enjoy the lake view, especially from the second-story study, and at the same time have privacy when using the pool. Around the pool and on the lawns privacy is assured not by the conventional courtyards of Palm Beach's 1920s mansions, but rather by angular walls extending from the house. Whereas a more traditional architect might have embellished the interior with columns or arches, Meier opted for a complicated yet appealing series of white steel beams. Instead of the more common stucco walls, he designed large expanses of clear glass to allow constant interaction between the interior and exterior spaces. "I try to create spaces where it is possible to be aware of the light at all times of the day," he says. In the bedrooms, narrow horizontal windows allow light in and ensure privacy at the same time.

A couple who have long been members of the Palm Beach community had observed the house being built and had developed a great affinity for it. When the opportunity arose for them to purchase it from the original owner, they didn't have to think twice. As soon as they bought the house they commissioned Meier to redo the interiors and design a new wing. It is not often that an architect has an opportunity to come back to a project once it is completed, so he welcomed the challenge with enthusiasm. "It is a house I would like to live in myself," Meier admits, bestowing an architect's greatest compliment.

BOHEMIAN BUNGALOW

The houses squeezed gable to gable between Sunrise Avenue and Atlantic Avenue make up Palm Beach's answer to Greenwich Village. The area  attracts established artists, as well as young, second-generation Palm Beachers who would rather buy a piece of local history than a more functional new house at the far north end of the island. This neighborhood was once called the Sticks, because of the simple wood-frame houses that originally stood here. Workers at Henry Morrison Flagler's massive wood-frame Royal Poinciana Hotel, opened in 1894, inhabited these modest quarters. Some historians claim that in order to rid the island of this disadvantaged set, Flagler invited them all to a circus in West Palm Beach. While they were gone, their houses mysteriously burned to the

Jolly took two days away from commissioned work to paint her own kitchen. On the floor she created a yellow and black checkered pattern and a trompe l'oeil blue area rug, the ends of which are curled. "It looks so real, even I tripped over it the first few days," she recalls. The cow painting is hers; the kitchen table came with the house.

Preceding pages
Left: Any stranger would know this seaside cottage belongs to artists. Walter Irving's artistic mirror frames of distressed gilt dot the lawn. Nancy Jolly's whimsical paintings hang on the front porch.
Right: Some of Palm Beach's most historic houses can be found on streets as unassuming as Root Trail.

ground. It is a strong accusation, even if apocryphal, because fires were a constant threat to the island. The original Breakers Hotel, a wooden structure that stood on the site of the current Breakers Hotel, a sprawling stucco building also owned by Flagler, was reduced to ashes on March 18, 1925.

At the heart of this neighborhood, hidden behind St. Edward's Parish Hall, is Root Trail. Like most blocks in the area, this street does not run from ocean to lake. Instead it is a short road, beginning at North County Road and ending at the ocean. Root Trail is reminiscent of a back street in Florida's most bohemian community, Key West. Its roof lines dip up and down; Victorian cottages stand next to boxy, New England–style shingle houses.

The street was named for Captain Enoch Root of Chicago. Before the turn of the century, Captain Root built a large estate on the lake a few hundred yards from where Root Trail is today. On the property he built small cottages, which he rented to artists. Daisy Erb, an artist and one of the cottage tenants, eventually bought the estate, which then became known as Daisy Erb's Artists' Colony.

A few years later Jane Peterson and Isabella Vernon Cook, well-known New York artists at the time, took a house in the colony. The two women encouraged the group to organize a formal showing and in 1918 the colony held its first joint exhibit, arranged by the art committee of Palm Beach's already established Women's Club. The show was a great success, artistically if not financially. But, since men could not join the Women's Club in those days, the art committee disassociated itself from the club and formed the Palm Beach County Art Club. By the mid-1920s, this once-small group had catapulted itself—

The owners call the modest
foyer of their beach cottage
the Great Hall, a reference
to the grand entrances of
oceanfront mansions that
sit just steps away.

Nancy Jolly, who styles her
house with other people's
castoffs, is always on the
lookout for paintings of
dogs, which she collects.

For the living room Jolly
procured this massive
mirror from an aunt's
house and painted the
edges. On the table are a
pair of Staffordshire dogs
inherited from a neighbor.
The strawberry-print sofa
and curtains were another
junk-store find.

and the town—into recognition as the art leaders of Florida. Thanks to private collections, fine commercial galleries, and the Norton Gallery of Art, that distinction remains valid today.

Nancy Jolly, an artist who was living in Los Angeles when she purchased the Palm Beach house in 1977, was almost mystically drawn to Root Trail. She bought the house on a whim while helping her aunt locate a place to rent. The realtor, with that innate sense of knowing a prospective buyer, took Jolly to see the seemingly run-down cottage. Entranced, Jolly then and there gave the realtor $1,000 in cash as a deposit on the boarded-up structure she had not yet entered.

When Jolly did get past the door, she discovered that the house was in perfect shape. "No one had ever modernized it so it wasn't desecrated. I painted it and moved in," says Jolly, who lived there with artist Walter Irving. Any stranger strolling past would have known the house belonged to artists. Irving created mirrors with geometric-patterned, distressed-gilt, hand-painted frames that usually rested on saw horses or leaned against palm trees in the front lawn to dry. Jolly painted murals in a studio upstairs, where she worked in oils and watercolors. She hung some of her fantastical paintings of exotic ladies and mythical animals with humorous, cartoonlike features on the front porch.

Jolly and Irving furnished the interior with treasures unearthed in junk stores. Jolly swears nothing was new "except the sheets and towels." The couple searched junk shops for six months before they found a dishwasher for twenty dollars. "It had never been used. It had a twenty-year-old instruction book and a free box of detergent," says Jolly, who considers it one of her better acquisitions.

She was even able to find a cheerful strawberry-print sofa with matching curtains for her living room. "It must be total intuition. Sometimes we take long shots and things don't work out," she says. One long shot that did work out was an old painting of a scruffy dog. Jolly and Irving dared each other to buy it. They lived with the picture for a while and it stole their hearts. Now several pictures of pups hang wherever the artists live.

Root Trail's history has come full circle. Around six o'clock every evening, as its residents emerge from their studios or return home from work, they always stop by one another's porches to see the latest rendering or to discuss block issues ranging from parking problems to the very name of the street. As in Daisy Erb's original colony, the artists on the street are friends. Over the years they have included internationally known silk-screen artist Thomas McKnight, local painter Connie Gasque, and Todd Draz, a renowned fashion artist who turned his talents to more interpretive painting. "Who would have thought we could have lived like this in Palm Beach?" says Jolly with a grin.

Above: Jolly almost always incorporates humor in her work. A nude of an exotic woman with a cartoonlike face hangs on the front porch. Left: This bathroom, which opens onto the front lawn, also serves as a beach cabana.

Nancy Jolly found every appliance in her kitchen at junk shops, including the dishwasher, which she bought for twenty dollars. The clock is from a school and the table came with the house.

MEDITERRANEAN MYSTIQUE

Addison Mizner, the legendary designer of Palm Beach's most fashionable houses and the man who gave the island its Mediterranean facade, had no academic credentials as an architect. At the age of forty-seven he qualified for a license to practice his profession under a grandfather clause that exempted those already working in the field from formal training. By the time Mizner came to Florida in 1918 he was already known for his ingenious designs and irresistible personal charm. Soon he was building resort homes for some of America's most socially prestigious families. By 1925, thanks to such lucrative commissions and a highly successful furniture-making business in West Palm Beach, Mizner had amassed a fortune, which he invested in an ambitious plan to develop Boca Raton, a town just south of Palm Beach, into a complete Mediterranean-style colony. The project failed after the market crashed, but Mizner had been so involved in it that he had declined any other commissions.

One of the last significant residences Mizner built in Palm Beach was for George S. Rasmussen, founder of the National Tea Company, a grocery-store chain based in Chicago. A Scandinavian, Rasmussen spent his summers outside of Copenhagen, but in the winter months he joined America's elite in their annual migration by private railroad car to Palm Beach. Mizner had built houses for many of Rasmussen's friends, including other Midwesterners such

as the Pillsburys and the McCormicks, so Rasmussen did not hesitate to commission the architect to build his house, knowing that a Mizner residence would confirm his social standing and provide the perfect backdrop for his collections of fine European paintings, tapestries, and Louis XIV and XV furnishings.

The house, originally named Casa Nana after Rasmussen's wife, is connected with one of the most colorful myths about Mizner. As the story goes, the architect forgot to include a staircase in the plans for Casa Nana. Realizing the mistake only after construction was under way, he improvised, designing a round, exterior stair tower gracefully punctuated by an open, stepped arcade. It was an enormous success, adding great distinction to the entrance of the house. Mizner's lack of a formal degree in architecture, abetted by his self-deprecating sense of humor, fed the legends that still surround his work. Indeed, the architect encouraged these legends as he realized that they only added to

Preceding pages
Left: The tower, with its spectacular spiral staircase, dominates the rear facade of the house.
Right: Interior of the spiral staircase, looking down.

Left: Interior of the spiral staircase, looking up.
Right: The upstairs loggia with its leaded-glass windows separates the master suite from the four guest suites and is renowned for its sweeping view of ocean to the east and lake to the west.

the original house. It has the same arched windows, curved capitals, red tile roof, and pale stucco facade. Also in the Mizner tradition is the loggia connecting the new room to the house.

Inside, Stedila created a breezy pavilion with a blue and white color scheme. Blue and white antique tiles from Portugal outline the arch of the French doors, and a white sofa stenciled with a hand-painted blue border is reflected in a contemporary glass coffee table. A pale stone Renaissance mantel frames the fireplace.

The French doors in the new room and in the loggia open onto a small Venetian-style garden that the owners use as an outdoor sitting area. Stedila and the owner found every tree and plant for the garden in a single day because they were determined to have it finished in time for the unveiling of the pavilion. Mizner, as legend has it, would paint oranges on clients' trees so that they would appear to be perfectly ripe. Stedila did not have to go to such extremes; his greenery was delivered in full bloom.

Stedila describes his efforts in the rest of the house as "a softening-up process." Upstairs, he designed a balcony for the master bedroom to bring in more light. For the massive living room, he found a nineteenth-century Aubusson rug and created a series of small sitting areas, so the room, which can accommodate many guests, would be equally comfortable for two people. "We wanted this to be a house, not a museum," explains Stedila. Indeed, he brought this stately mansion back to life.

The downstairs loggia
commands a spectacular
view of the ocean.

The new room, designed by
Palm Beach architect Jeff
Smith, is on the same grand
scale as the original house,
but its comfortable interior
provides a casual option to
the formality of the other
rooms.

HEAVENLY HAVEN

In 1974 Mimi McMakin moved into Palm Beach's first church, Bethesda-by-the-Sea. The simple, shingle-style building, constructed in 1894, sits on Lake Worth and in the early days parishioners arrived at the waterfront church by boat. But on April 12, 1925, its last services were held and its swelling congregation moved to an imposing Gothic-style stone building at the corner of South County Road and Barton Avenue. The bells in the old church's tower may no longer summon parishioners, but the tower's grand, now inoperative, Seth Thomas clock fascinates those who spot it from the nearby bicycle path.

Fifteen years after the church was closed, the Maddocks, one of Palm Beach's earliest families, annexed the building and it became part of what is

The arched door of the morning porch leads to the front walkway, which is lined with orchids hanging from citrus trees. Green and pink Cowtan & Tout fabrics cover the breakfast table and chairs; hats and plants contribute to the room's buoyant feeling.

Preceding pages
Left: The narrow hallway leading from the morning porch to the lakeside veranda is decorated with navigation charts, flags from yachting clubs in the Bahamas, and colorful signal flags. Right: Palm Beach's first church, Bethesda-by-the-Sea, built in 1894, sits on the Intracoastal Waterway. The simple shingle-style building and its gabled roof boasts a bell tower with a filigreed metal Seth Thomas clock.

Left: The shingles on the lakeside veranda were left their natural brown and covered with Maddock family souvenirs, including Mimi's brother's childhood train set. Deep green and rose Brunschwig & Fils fabrics cover the natural-colored wicker furniture.

now the Maddock family compound. The grounds contain many of the island's historic houses, including Maddock Tree Tops, Twigs, the Song House, and Duck's Nest. Brought from Brooklyn, New York, by barge in 1891, Duck's Nest is the oldest island house continuously owned by the same family.

The church became Mimi McMakin's residence when the native Palm Beacher returned to the island for a month's visit. A month became a year and, as she began adding her personal touches to the place, it became obvious that Mimi was there to stay. Ironically, the house of Mimi's dreams is the same house that instilled fear in her as a child. She grew up in Maddock Tree Tops (her great-grandfather was Henry Maddock) and her bedroom window faced the gloomy church. To avoid seeing the spooky place, she constantly kept her shades drawn. Once Mimi decided to live in the church, she immediately started brightening up the rooms while retaining the building's original charm. "I wasn't quite sure what church style was, but the church was very dark and it needed something whimsical," says Mimi, who was an interior designer in New York before establishing Kemble

The small kitchen required little structural change. A local artist's trompe l'oeil painting of family pets covers the cabinets.

Cool green and white Portuguese tiles replaced rugs on the morning porch. Whitewashed shutters close off the interior window to the kitchen; a mirror beside it reflects the outdoors. Wicker furniture and an heirloom carved Chinese desk that Mimi's great-grandmother brought here by steamship in the 1850s were painted white to enhance the room's sunny disposition.

Interiors in Palm Beach with partner Brooke Huttig.

Mimi left the church's dominating nave intact and it serves as a catchall for a family that throws little away. When her daughters, Celerie and Phoebe, were younger, the nave was an ideal club house where they could have slumber parties and chase each other on roller skates. Part of the nave has been turned into a cozy corner where the family can watch movies in the evenings.

Days are spent on the house's two porches, the arcades of which Mimi closed in to provide breezy living space. She painted the interior cypress shingles of the morning porch a soft pink. The wood was so porous that it required seven coats of paint. She replaced rugs with soothing green and white Portuguese tiles, and courageously painted her great-grandmother's Victorian furniture white. Cheerful pink and green Cowtan & Tout fabrics cover sofas, cushions, and table skirts. Large mirrors on the interior wall reflect the outdoor greenery.

From the morning porch a walkway accented with occasional orchids hanging from citrus trees leads to the front of the house,

The church nave with exposed rafters serves as a storage space. A screen painted in a lattice pattern and potted palms serve to delineate an intimate dining area within the spacious room.

which is blanketed with flame vines and assorted varieties of hibiscus. Gardening tools and bicycles lie about and a hammock hangs in a shady spot near the latest addition—a hot tub Mimi gave her husband for his birthday.

The small kitchen, installed fifty years ago, required few changes. A local artist painted the cabinets in trompe l'oeil, incorporating some details of family history, including pets, past and present. "The only animal in the painting we haven't had is the pig," says Mimi, laughing.

A deep-arched veranda runs along the lake side of the house. "The lake porch is a hodgepodge of things we love," says Mimi, who commissioned another local artist to paint vignettes on the doors leading to the nave. A light-colored sisal rug, its edges hand-stenciled, lies under comfy sofas and chairs covered with deep green and rose fabrics. The church's original stained-glass windows were framed with plywood shutters on which morning glories and hyacinths are painted. Decorations ranging from a sack made of paper-thin tree bark and fishing poles to a well-hugged Raggedy Ann doll and empty bird cages make this porch a cozy spot. The morning porch and the lakeside veranda are connected by a narrow hallway decorated with souvenir navigation charts and yachting flags from sea voyages made by Mimi's husband, Leigh.

Although bathrooms tend to be far away from bedrooms, and minuscule closets—originally designed to hold the parson's robes—are not always adequate for the wardrobes of a mother and two daughters, the happiness this house brings to Mimi and her family far outweighs any architectural quirks—even a leaning bell tower takes on charm.

In the octagonally shaped master bedroom, situated at the base of the bell tower, a secretary showcases a collection of nineteenth–century English thatched cottage china tea caddies and coffeepots by John Maddock and Sons (Mimi's great-grandfather).

SCAVENGER'S REWARD

*P*aul Prosperi once bought the least expensive house he could find in Palm Beach. "People say you need glamour in Palm Beach and I wanted to prove you didn't," says Prosperi, who paid less than $200,000  for an undistinguished north-end residence and with creative audacity turned it into a showplace that became the envy of his friends. Among his more memorable additions were a four-toned peach privacy wall and surrealistic pool steps extending out of the water into midair. "By the time I was ready to sell the house, people were lined up to buy it," says the affable attorney. Prosperi soon tackled another design challenge—organizing livable space out of two identical buildings and a small loggia, all joined by a narrow, crumbling brick pathway. The residence, designed by architect Belford Shoumate, sits in a cul-de-sac originally called Circle Plaza but renamed Phipps Plaza when it was developed, in 1925, by John S. Phipps. Over the years noted Palm Beach architects such as Addison Mizner, Maurice Fatio, John

Volk, Howard Major, and Belford Shoumate have added to it. The charming plaza—now filled with quaint office space occupied primarily by companies in the building trade, including architects, contractors, interior designers, and engineers, was the first district to be designated a historic landmark by the Palm Beach Landmarks Commission.

"Belford Shoumate was basically a scavenger," observes Prosperi. The loggia is an example of the architect's secret passion for scrounging. Its framework is in fact the skeleton of an open-air structure that was once part of Bradley's Beach Club, Palm Beach's swankest dinner club and casino. Owned by Edward R. "Colonel" Bradley, the club was operated illegally from the day it opened in 1898 to the day it shut down in 1946.

Palm Beach was never richer than in the pre-income tax days, and there was no limit to the amount of money that would change hands at Bradley's. Harvey Firestone, Josh Cosden, Flo Ziegfeld, Harry Payne Whitney, and John Studebaker were reputed to have each lost as much as $300,000 in a single night at the tables.

The Colonel did not approve of gambling by those who couldn't afford to lose. Members were chosen carefully, recommended by other members, but ultimately approved by Bradley, who knew the exact worth of every guest. In Cleveland Amory's book *The Last Resorts*, the well-known story is told of a woman who entered the casino one day in tears, claiming that she and her husband had lost their entire savings of $5,000. Bradley thought

In the cozy, brick-walled dining room, eighteenth-century Italian chairs surround a modern table designed by English furniture maker Anthony Redmile. An eighteenth-century Venetian tapestry hangs over the fireplace. The pedestal, by American sculptor Albert Paley, supports a vase designed in the 1920s by Mizner.

Preceding pages
Left: These identical bungalows were separate residences until Prosperi united them. In one house is a living room and dining room; the other has a bedroom and study. The buildings, joined by a small walkway, were designed by architect Belford Shoumate, whose own house was next door. Right: The roof tiles are from a Phipps family estate, probably Casa Bendita, which has been torn down. Most likely these tiles were made in Mizner's workshop in West Palm Beach.

Right: The living room is decorated in a witty blend of styles. On the Victorian tray table an antique hammered silver vase by Mario Buccelati sits next to hand sculptures made of balsa wood with gold and silver leaf by Pedro Friedeberg. A Matisse drawing of Pan and a tapestry created for Louis XIV's coronation flank the doorway.

Left: The study is designed around Prosperi's eclectic collection of furniture and art. An 1850 Victorian sofa is still covered in its original leather. An early twentieth-century table by Austrian architect Adolf Loos sits on a nineteenth-century Native American rug. A David Hockney drawing hangs above the eighteenth-century Irish pine mantelpiece. Against the far wall is a wicker daybed from Conran's London design store.

Below: On the cluttered bookshelves in Prosperi's study is Arnold Newman's photographic portrait of Igor Stravinsky.

for a minute, handed her five $1,000 bills, and made her promise never to enter the club again. The next night the colonel saw her husband and approached him. "You were told never to come here again. You can't afford this and your wife agreed." "But Colonel," he said, "I'm not married." The man was the son of Harvey Firestone. The colonel decided, "Anyone who could get the best of an old dog like me earned the $5,000."

When nights at the posh establishment finally ended, Joseph Kennedy, Sr., gave this eulogy to a society columnist: "Palm Beach lost all of its zipperoo." The scion of the Kennedy clan

Shoumate scavenged the skeleton of this loggia from the remains of Bradley's Beach Club, Palm Beach's illegal casino, which ran until 1946. Prosperi installed a floor and had French doors designed to fit the mismatched arches of the open-air structure. He furnished it with an exotic mixture of Thai elephant chairs, an eighteenth-century English sofa, kilim rugs, and French posters from the 1920s.

On the table to the left of the four-poster bed is a sketch by Renoir of his son Claude. On the table to the right is a David Hockney pen-and-ink drawing.

maintained a friendship with Colonel Bradley even though Bradley astutely sold Kennedy his considerable interest in Hialeah Race Park only a few hours before President Roosevelt issued a war order closing all tracks for the duration of World War II in order to economize on gasoline.

Thanks to Shoumate's penchant for scavenging, a remnant of the colorful history of Bradley's Beach Club lives on as a part of Paul Prosperi's former residence. He had custom windows and doors designed to accommodate the loggia's aging and mismatched arches. "It was no easy trick," he recalls, but he felt it was worth the headache because it gave the house a sunroom.

When Prosperi lived there, each of the two identical houses served a specific function. The southern house incorporated a bedroom filled with personal clutter and a study where floor-to-ceiling bookshelves flanked a well-worn brown leather sofa. The kitchen was rarely used to make anything more complicated than coffee, as Prosperi cooked in the northern house when entertaining.

The front door of the northern house opens onto a steep, narrow staircase that leads to the second floor, which Prosperi fashioned into a small sitting area furnished in an eclectic style. On the ground floor is a cozy dining room and a well-stocked kitchen.

The arrangement of the buildings, if quirky, seemed natural and practical. Prosperi could easily have been the only person in Palm Beach whose one-bedroom residence had four baths, four terraces, four fireplaces, and two kitchens.

Above and left: The chair seen at left (and reflected in the mirror) is from the ocean liner *Normandy* and adds to the drama of this sleek bathroom.

GEORGIAN REDUX

*T*here isn't a prominent street in Palm Beach that doesn't lead to a house designed by architect John Volk. Volk emigrated to the United States from Graz, Austria, when he was ten years old. He graduated  from Columbia University and worked in New York before opening an office in Palm Beach. Although he is best remembered for his private residences, some of the one thousand projects he undertook throughout his career were plans for entire communities, including Old Port Cove and Lost Tree Village, both in Palm Beach County, and Paradise Island in Nassau. He also designed Palm Beach's Royal Poinciana Plaza, home of the nightclub Au Bar and the more sedate Royal Poinciana Theater, in which Volk incorporated a seventy-ton roof that slides open in four minutes. One of his last public commissions was Good Samaritan Hospital in West Palm Beach. When Volk first arrived in Palm Beach, Mediterranean-style houses were the prevailing trend. He proved masterful at this style, and three of his grandest efforts may be seen at 191 Banyan Way, 190 South Ocean Boulevard, and 343 El Brillo Way, all in the estate area at the southern

end of the island. But with the decline of
the Florida land boom, already under way
by the stock market crash in 1929, these
Mediterranean Revival houses became
prohibitively expensive to build.

In James R. Knott's *The Mansion Builders*,
there is an essay on John Volk by W. R.
Selmier, who states that a Mediterranean
house in those days cost $2.50 per square
foot, as opposed to ordinary mansions,
which could be built for 50 cents a square foot, because the
Mediterranean style entailed elaborate castings, carvings, tiles,
and imported furniture. Volk's wife, Jane, says Volk realized that
building such houses was impossible, but he also noted that many
people were coming to live in Palm Beach year round, bringing
their northern Federal furniture with them. So Volk went off to
the Caribbean and Bermuda, where Colonial designs had already
been adapted to the subtropical climate.

Upon his return from the islands, Volk built a Bermuda house
for himself, which he called White Gables. As the story goes, Volk
once spotted a car in town with the name White Gables painted
on its side. He followed the driver of the car home, stopped him
in the driveway, and said, "I notice you have named your house
White Gables. That is the name of my house and as an architect I
can't help but notice your house has a hip roof, so I am wondering
if you could change the name of your house to White Hips." The
man Volk confronted was Clifford Browkaw, who eventually
commissioned Volk to design a house for him.

Volk continued building modified renditions of Colonial,

Preceding pages
**Left: White wooden gates
and a brick walkway lead to
a magnificent slat house on
a neighboring lot north of
the house. The addition was
a gift from the man of the
house to his wife, who loves
to spend entire days there
tending flowers, especially
her orchids. It was
designed by Leta Austin
Foster and Jackie Albarran,
a Palm Beach architect.
Right: This iron putti adorns
a border of greenery on the
lakefront side of the house.**

**Left: Climbing vines
transform the otherwise
nondescript wall enclosing
the pool into an attractive
design element.
Right: A columned terrace
off the dining room looks
onto the pool, which is
presided over by a ceramic
pelican.**

especially Georgian, houses. During the late 1930s and early 1940s he designed a particularly pretty cluster of Colonial houses on a midtown lakeside block. Some have a Monterey influence while others incorporate lacy New Orleans–style ironwork on the verandas. The buyers of these houses, which were built on speculation, included Mr. and Mrs. James Ballantine, Mr. and Mrs. Milton Fuller, the race car driver Mr. Briggs Cunningham and his wife, and Matthew Mellon of the Pittsburgh banking family.

In 1950 Henry Gibson moved from a house two doors down into one of Volk's Georgian-style houses right on the lake. In it Volk modified traditional Georgian design by incorporating floor-to-ceiling windows, plantation shutters that slid into the wall when opened, and breezy verandas. Gibson lived there until his death at age 102, when the current owners bought the house from his estate.

At the time decorator Leta Austin Foster lived next door to the Gibson estate. When she heard the lakefront house was available, she immediately called a girlhood friend and insisted that she and her husband take a look at it. The couple, who had an apartment in Palm Beach's Lowell House, had no intention of owning a house in Florida, but Volk's design appealed to their Southern origins, and they found themselves planning simple structural changes while looking at the house.

Naturally, they called upon Foster to handle the remodeling. Foster, whose former house was built in the same style, respected the original design and made few changes. She was also happy to incorporate some of the handsome eighteenth-century English antiques Gibson had left behind.

Left: Stately Georgian touches in the house include these shell moldings in the living room. But Volk modified the Georgian design with generous floor-to-ceiling windows and plantation shutters that slide into the walls. Leta Foster chose a lightweight white fabric from Brunschwig & Fils for the draperies.

The entrance hall originally had grand proportions but few embellishments. The owners added woodwork and moldings to the curved staircase. An eighteenth-century English fish-eye mirror that belonged to Henry Gibson, the original owner of the house, hangs over an eighteenth-century English sideboard.

On the west side of the
house, near a curve in the
bicycle path, is a gazebo. In
it, a painting by William
Benjamin depicts how the
curve might have looked in
the 1920s. The lake is lined
with palm trees instead of
houses and a boat house
sits at the end of the dock,
as many did at that time.

Foster did emphasize the subtropical adaptations Volk had made. She extended the front veranda slightly to accommodate outdoor dining. The back veranda was closed in with French doors but the original brick floor was retained. Bay windows were added to the back of the house to provide a more expansive view of the lake.

Other changes disguise the pared-down construction typical of the post–World War II era. The stairway, for example, was customized with beautiful wooden handrails and moldings. The owners wanted a gazebo by their pool but town ordinances prohibited building another structure on the property. Foster cleverly solved the problem by fashioning a gazebo, complete with electricity and running water, out of a bomb shelter topped by a small observatory that Mr. Gibson, an amateur astronomer, had built.

The current owners are avid gardeners. He is an established authority on daffodils. Recently, she was given a slat house for Christmas. "I have so few days to just stay here and garden," she says. "I am the happiest when I have a whole day to work in my slat house."

dining room. The kitchen wing ran along the southern side of the house.

Biddle was active in the Palm Beach social scene. His father was the inspiration for the book *The Happiest Millionaire* and Tony was not far behind. An ace tennis player, he was a charter member of the Bath and Tennis Club and served as the club's first president. He also founded the less exclusive Oasis Club and helped finance the town's first and only movie house, the Paramount Theater. These three buildings had one thing in common: they were all designed by architect Joseph Urban.

In 1927 Biddle hired Urban to remodel Villa del Sarmiento. Urban moved the entrance to the ocean side and turned the old dining room into the entrance hall. Placing a new, grander dining room further to the south, he remodeled the former kitchen wing into a large patio and demolished Madame Gais's house next door, to make room for a new kitchen and service rooms.

But neither Urban nor Molyneux disturbed the Mizner flavor of cloistered courtyards, Gothic archways, and pale stucco facade. As Molyneux became better acquainted with the house, he grew to appreciate the sophistication of Mizner's irreverent, dramatic themes. It wasn't long before he became Mizner's modern-day accomplice, incorporating flights of fancy into the remodeling. He began by chipping away at the house in search of the original

The living room ceiling is painted in Baroque style. On the wall to the left, above a sofa upholstered in a Manuel Canovas velvet, is Picasso's **Homme assis au verre (1941). To the right of the fireplace is Francis Bacon's *Figure Turning*. Armchairs are by Sylvain Nicholas Blanchard (1743).**

plan; he removed sliding glass doors, obstructive partitions, and the central staircase balustrade. Since Mizner's original plan for the second floor was no longer clear, Molyneux gutted it and created two large suites with palatial marble baths and dressing rooms.

Downstairs the designer left two large pillars that most likely had separated the living room and an outdoor patio, which is now closed in. He refashioned the former patio as a casual living space and decorated the living room more formally, using rich silks and velvets, but he kept the colors light to avoid too sharp a contrast with the adjoining room.

In the library Molyneux chose pecky cypress, a wood that was often used in Mizner's day, for the paneling. He combed antique stores for iron fixtures made by the Mizner workshop and used them throughout the house. Otherwise he counted on dramatic murals and trompe l'oeil paintings to match wits with Mizner. "Where Mizner would have used embellishments like gar–goyles and brackets, I used paint," says Molyneux, who turned to the owners' collection of works by Pablo Picasso, Francis Bacon, Henry Moore, and Helen Frankenthaler for inspiration. In a chancy move, Molyneux commissioned a mural for the stairwell that incorporates details from Old Master paintings of the Spanish school as well as works in the owners' collection. The gamble paid off. "The clients understood," he says. And Mizner would have applauded.

Left: On the wall of the stairwell is a daring trompe l'oeil painting by Robert Archer and Emma Temple depicting distorted renderings of important works in the owners' art collection as well as details from Old Master paintings.

Above: A bronze by Marino Marini sits on a seventeenth-century Spanish table in the library. Manuel Canovas velvet velour is used on the walls. The rug is nineteenth-century Chinese. A flame-pattern Clarence House fabric covers the club chairs. Miró's *Peinture* (1933), Picasso's *Femme dans un fauteuil* (1939), and Chagall's *La Chambre jaune* (1922) decorate the walls.

Below: In the daughter's bedroom the trompe l'oeil ceiling was painted by Lucrezia Moroni. Clarence House fabrics are draped on the iron four-poster bed and used on furniture throughout the room. An Art Deco mirror by Edgar Brandt hangs over the Louis XV chair. The rug depicts Europa astride the bull, surrounded by the twelve golden stars of the European flag; it was designed by Nigel Coates in 1990 and is called "L'Europea."

THE VICARAGE

*I*n 1975 the Preservation Foundation of Palm Beach, established to protect historic architecture, designated the beloved Vicarage as the town's first landmark  house. Originally built for the first vicar of the episcopal church Bethesda-by-the-Sea, it is the third oldest residence on the island. Its simple turn-of-the-century clapboard style appealed immensely to one-time resident Douglas Fairbanks, Jr.—son of the swashbuckling silent film star and a knighted actor in his own right—and his late wife, Mary Lee, who was once married to A&P grocery store heir Huntington Hartford. "It didn't seem to compete with the big mansions and it had a reasonable amount of room. Aside from being the third oldest house on the island it wasn't significant architecturally, but it was well built and conveniently located," Fairbanks recalls.

Eileen Fairchild, who bought the Vicarage from Fairbanks in 1989, thought everything about it was thoroughly charming, although it was in sore need of rewiring and new plumbing. "No one had touched it in quite a while. One bolt of lightning would have sent it to the sky!" she says. Mrs. Fairchild enlisted Palm Beach designer Lillian Fernandez. Both Lillian, who grew up in Palm Beach, and Mrs. Fairchild knew the house from its Fairbanks days. They were determined to update the historical site without banishing the laid-back charm established by the island's original inhabitants and continued by the Fairbankses. "I wanted to bring the house up to the 1990s standard of living, but in doing so I wanted to be true to the historical heritage of the house," Mrs. Fairchild says. That history included many notable visitors in the Fairbankses' time. The king and queen of Romania arrived unannounced one

morning, sending the Fairbankses scurrying upstairs from the porch to change out of their bathrobes. Princess Margaret often visited for tea, but never unannounced.

The Fairbankses' sable brown dining room seated only eight, but the guest list was always impressive: Great Britain's nuclear scientist Lord Solly Zuckerman; English novelist Barbara Cartland; Senator and Mrs. Jacob Javits; Sotheby's Palm Beach representative and former *House and Garden* columnist Lou Gartner; the Duke and Duchess of Wellington; Estée Lauder; Palm Beach philanthropists Mr. and Mrs. Nate Appleman; the Earl of Westmorland; Grace Mirabella; neighbors Princess Maria Pia and Prince Michel de Bourbon Parme; His Honor Rajamata of

Preceding pages
Left: The inviting lakeside porch overlooks the pool, which the Fairbankses dubbed the Lagoon.
Right: A hand-painted ceramic bas-relief depicting the Madonna and child hangs on the terrace wall.

Above: Built for Palm Beach's first resident vicar at the turn of the century, the Vicarage is a modest New England–style clapboard house.
Right: The pecky cypress of the living room walls was carefully restored because the wood, once abundant on the island, is now rather rare. Overstuffed sofas are covered in a floral-patterned Scalamandré fabric.

Right: The pergola is a
favorite lunch spot.
Ralph Lauren wicker
chaises longues flank a
table surrounded by
1930s bamboo chairs.

During renovation, every
opportunity was taken to
bring in light; even these
kitchen shelves are backed
by a window.

Jaipur; TV commentator Herbert Bayard Swope; astronaut Edgar
Mitchell; and Lord Laurence Olivier and Lady Olivier (Joan
Plowright), whom Fairbanks considered "my oldest and dearest
friends." Olivier was a frequent house guest even though the
Vicarage was, as Fairbanks admits, "quite deliberately limited in
its accommodation for parties or for flocks of house guests."

That changed when Mrs. Fairchild set about restyling the house.
Since her four daughters and one son-in-law visited often, she gave
Lillian the basic mission of creating more living space. Along with
Palm Beach architect Jeff Smith, Lillian turned an outbuilding,
previously used as a garage, into a bachelor's quarters. The
original butler's residence, off of the kitchen, became a wing of
bedrooms for the daughters, who referred to it as "the dormitory."

The upstairs functioned as a separate house where the owner
escaped from the madness of spring breaks. Lillian and Jeff turned
two upstairs bedrooms into a spacious lakeside master suite with a
sitting area and grand bathroom. French doors lead from the suite
to an outdoor balcony. One other bedroom was converted into a
library, while still another was left as a guest room.

Consumed with the project, Lillian went as far as sewing table
skirts and lace draperies herself, finishing the entire house in an
amazing six months. The extraordinary efforts of Lillian, Mrs.
Fairchild, and Jeff Smith were instantly recognized. In 1990 the
Preservation Foundation of Palm Beach honored Mrs. Fairchild
with the Robert I. Ballinger award in recognition of excellence in
restoration, and Lillian swears this restoration will suffice for the
next ninety years.

ALL HANDS ON DECO

"One man in our family worked hard and made a fortune, enabling the rest of us to pursue our artistic dreams," Kirby Kooluris says candidly of his great-grandfather, who amassed his wealth operating theaters during the days of dream in 1982, when he and his an Art Deco house on Palm that is now filled with his family's passionately restoring it to its  concession stands in New York vaudeville. Kooluris realized his wife, Joan, bought Fore and Aft, Beach's Intracoastal Waterway works. Since then he has been original design, going as far as soaking door handles and lighting fixtures in vinegar for a week to obtain the perfect coloring. The house is deserving of such ardent attention. It was designed by architect Belford Shoumate in 1937 and won the House of the Future award at New York's 1939 World's Fair. It also earned the distinction of being the first Art Deco residence in Palm Beach to be designated a historical landmark.

Although Shoumate did design more conservative houses, he was well versed in Deco. Educated at the progressive New School, he worked for a time under Joseph Urban, whom he helped to design Manhattan's Radio City Music Hall, a splendid example of American Art Deco architecture.

At the time the house was built, the north end of the island had not yet been developed and the area was filled with thick foliage. Shoumate's budget was unlimited; the only aesthetic requirement was that the house resemble a ship. Kooluris recalls Shoumate saying that he never had the privilege of so much free reign in his work again.

In 1982 a prominent Palm Beach attorney who has a penchant for unique houses and also owns a house designed by Shoumate tipped Kirby off that the residence was about to go on the market. "I told him to go see it with a check in his hand. I couldn't stand the thought that someone I didn't know would be living there," recalls the lawyer. Kirby describes the house when he first saw it as looking like "a fraternity on a Sunday morning." He remembers that some of his friends could not understand what he wanted with a house whose exterior design included wavelike moldings and the symbol of a Ford V8.

Kooluris's family built and still owns a famous Art Nouveau house in Hunter, New York. Originally called the Dream Garden and now called Woodlands, it was designed by Kirby's great-uncle Nathan Dolinsky, who also painted enormous allegorical panels specifically for it. Dolinsky exhibited along with the French Impressionists at New York's 1913 Armory Show. When Kooluris inherited the paintings he knew they would need a special backdrop. "The Dream Garden looks very

Below: The narrow, winding stairway has a low ceiling like that of a ship. A pen-and-ink drawing by Kooluris's uncle Dr. Richard Stark hangs on the wall.

Preceding pages Left and right: Designed in 1937, Fore and Aft celebrates the ocean liners of the day. Its sleekly curving and slender design makes use of every inch of its small, 65-foot-wide lot, accommodating five bed–room suites, each with its own balcony, a loggia, a living room, and a dining room.

Right: Glass brick, often used in Art Deco design, allows light into the bedroom and bathroom of this guest suite. A wide doorway joining the two narrow rooms makes them feel spacious. The large painted screen is one of the many works in the house by Kirby Kooluris's great-uncle Nathan Dolinsky.

Right: Shoumate incorporated the unmistakable symbol of a Ford V8, an invention of the 1930s, into a window on the side of the house as a fanciful motif.

Left: In the living room a portholelike window is flanked on the left by a portrait of Kooluris's great-aunt Blossom Dolinsky, a silent film actress, and on the right by a portrait of his great aunt Aida Kotlarsky, a concert pianist. Both were painted by Nathan Dolinsky. The furniture was all designed by Shoumate for the house. Polish pianist Paderewski gave concerts on this piano. It is said that he had a pet alligator whose favorite nesting place was on this coffee table.

Above: Kooluris inherited this portrait of his great-aunt Blossom from the artist, his great-uncle Nathan Dolinsky.

much like this house on a bigger scale. What other house in Palm Beach would be crazy enough for these paintings?" he asks.

Dolinsky often painted Kooluris's family, including his mother, Hortense Kooluris, the longest-surviving of Isadora Duncan's dance students. There is an Arnold Genthe photograph of her in Kirby's living room that won a first prize in photography at the 1939 World's Fair. Paintings by Kooluris's sister, Linda Dobbs, are also scattered throughout the house, as are pen-and-ink drawings by his uncle Dr. Richard Stark, who is considered a pioneer in plastic surgery and whose art has been exhibited alongside Robert Motherwell's.

After moving into the house, Kooluris discovered that Polish pianist and statesman Ignace Jan Paderewski had lived there during World War II and gave concerts in the house for the Polish Relief Fund. Paderewski gave his last Palm Beach performance in 1941 at El Mirasol, Eva Stotesbury's house, which no longer stands. The concert was staged by Mrs. Charles Merrill (then Princess Salstem-Zalessky) and Mrs. William Randolph Hearst, who flew Metropolitan opera star Richard Crooks from New York for the event. Eleanor Roosevelt also attended the concert, impressing Paderewski by receiving him at El Mirasol without pomp or circumstance. Kooluris continues the Paderewski tradition by presenting small concerts for friends, whose original skepticism about the house has abated, most probably because of Kooluris's infectious enthusiasm.

The house's sleek lines and round windows are all typically

Left: This second–floor bathroom, with its porthole–shaped mirror and window, connects to two of the guest suites.

Right: This narrow loggia serves as an entrance gallery. The two-panel screen was painted by the owner's great-uncle Nathan Dolinsky.

Deco. Shoumate also incorporated the romantic side of Deco design, displaying a fascination with the future, especially transportation. With its curved lines and its three increasingly narrow stories, the house bears a distinct resemblance to an ocean liner. Like ship's cabins, each of the five upstairs suites has a terrace and private entrance. A narrow exterior walkway runs along the top floor, the upper molding of which is fashioned in a wave pattern. The roof is flat, another Deco feature, and can be used as an observation deck to watch real boats go by on Lake Worth.

Kooluris chose not to restore the house's exterior to its original cobalt blue, to the great relief of his neighbors. "The town enacted a color code because of this house," Kooluris says. But he is fanatical about retaining the original stark interior design, which others might have eagerly but mistakenly rushed to warm up. Intact are chairs, dressers, built-in breakfast trays, and a maple parquet floor that Kooluris discovered under black linoleum installed by a previous owner. He even uses dinner plates from the 1939 New York World's Fair, found by a friend.

When Kooluris installed a swimming pool he paid custom-design prices because he wanted it to be raised and have the same sleek lines as the house. Although the house also has an oceanfront cabana, next he would like to build a dock on the Intracoastal. "I use every bit of my money on this house, and everyone who visits has had some input." While these additions make the house more suitable to Kooluris's lifestyle, they are mere conveniences; it is the original design that inspires and obsesses him. "Can you believe this was going on in the jungle in 1937?" he asks.

FANTASY COTTAGE

$\mathcal{B}$efore the turn of the century, Palm Beach was known as the Lake Worth Cottage Colony. At that time, most of the island's buildings were modest wood-  frame beach cottages. With the 1920s came the grand mansions for which the town is still famous. Then in the 1930s vacationers again began building residences in the island's relaxed resort style. One of these simple structures, built in 1935, has evolved, almost under its own will, into one of Palm Beach's prettiest settings. The owners bought the somewhat neglected house as a temporary lodging while they shopped for a permanent residence. "It was very sweet and charming but there were things we wanted to do to make it more comfortable while we were here," says the wife. The couple called on longtime friend and architect Henry Melich of Nassau, who began making small changes and gradually tailored the house to suit

Preceding pages
Left: Detail of the exquisite eighteenth-century grotto-style bas-relief that is housed in a tiny latticework pavilion at the end of the back lawn.
Right: A small pavilion located at the end of a striking blue-tiled pool provides respite from the sun. A topiary tree marks the entrance to the enclosed garden in back of the house.

A wall decorated with a trompe l'oeil urn and masonry was built between the guest house and the main house. Beams were added to give this open space the illusion of being a bona fide room.

Left: The gazebo is where the couple prefers to entertain. During the day, sunlight filters in through the slatted wooden roof, casting shadows in basket-weave patterns on the table and cane-backed chairs. Gardenia bushes planted nearby provide a constant sweet scent during parties.

them perfectly. "Every time we did think of moving we couldn't possibly sell the house because it was always torn to bits," says the wife, who has lived here happily for over ten years. Now the welcoming cottage has become a compound of sorts, incorporating a separate guest house, two walled gardens, a blue-tiled pool with a pavilion, and a magical gazebo.

The whole process began when the couple requested a proper front hall. Melich removed a powder room to create space for a new entrance and hallway. The original entrance was converted into a living room window that looks onto a garden in front of the house where narrow brick walkways are lined with citrus trees in large terra-cotta pots. This garden is concealed from the street by walls of dense hedges.

The house continued to evolve as walls were torn down to create comfortable, livable space out of an old-fashioned, mazelike arrangement. Downstairs a wall was extended ten feet to form a breakfast room and enlarge the dining room. Upstairs two generous bedrooms were designed and the original sleeping porch was transformed into a sitting room adjoining the master bedroom.

Interior designer Imogene Taylor of Colefax & Fowler gave the cottage a subtle Victorian flavor that suited the couple, who have a house in London, perfectly. In the living room chintz drapes and upholstery in brisk shades of green and yellow contrast cheerfully with the soothing blue, striated walls. Softly rounded sofas and chairs are decoratively skirted. An L-shaped banquette

A powder room was removed to create this entrance hall. The low table is decorated with small topiary plants. A graceful swan planter, filled with the house's surrounding greenery, is a garden in itself.

sofa defines the main sitting area and allows room for two additional sitting areas in an otherwise small space. Brass door handles here and in every other room constantly gleam, adding to the house's sunny atmosphere.

Off the living room is a loggia dominated by two bridge tables. This bright yellow room, adorned with botanical prints and tulip-patterned fabrics, is a perfect spot for a woman who divides her leisure time between playing bridge and enjoying her gardens, which are visible from the room.

Twenty-seven truckloads of jungle growth were removed from the back of the house to reveal a sizable lawn. This came as a pleasant surprise to the couple, who had no idea it was so large. After clearing away swampy ground created by storm water that had been left standing in the back for some time, Henry Melich created a walkway to the area, where the owners fashioned a courtyard enclosed by hedges. Inside the courtyard, a narrow

A brightly patterned chintz adds a lively touch to the living room, with its pale blue, striated walls and slightly darker blue, geometrically patterned rug. Banquette sofas and settees maximize the seating capacity of this cozy, subtly Victorian room.

brick path leads to a cutting garden, an herb garden, a small reflecting pond, and rows of tall orchids. "It was fun to see the seedlings sprout," says the owner, who is an active member of the Palm Beach Garden Club. She used to enter flower shows (which often meant waking up at four in the morning to have her flowers to a judge by five) but now only participates in the town's exhibits. Her favorite flowers are David Austin's old-fashioned English roses, the seeds for which she acquired from a grower in England. As the roses bloom perpetually, small bouquets of them can always be found throughout the house.

At the far end of the garden is a small lattice pavilion where orchids are occasionally housed. An enchanting bas-relief of a mermaid in eighteenth-century grotto style adorns the wall of the pavilion. Just to the right, a topiary monkey hanging from a citrus tree marks the entrance to a tropical garden. The couple began cultivating this garden only recently, after a date palm fell down, leaving the area bare. "When we originally planted the gardens I was in more of an English period," says the owner, who now confesses to thoughts of a house on a tropical island in the middle of the sea. Along the walkway in the tropical garden are various sorts of palm trees, banana trees, and riotously flowering hibiscus.

Closer to the house is a magnificent high arched gazebo, where the couple prefers to entertain. During the day, sunlight filters through the slatted roof, creating an enchanting basket-weave pattern in the outdoor room. During the evening, the doors of the house are left wide open to the gazebo, the pool, and the surrounding gardens, bringing the outdoors inside and creating a perfect harmony between the two.

Above: A small guest house has vaulted ceilings with beams painted a misty blue. Antique iron beds have been painted in the same refreshing color. The window overlooks the tropical garden.

Left: The loggia serves as a bridge room. Tulip prints hanging on the bright yellow walls as well as tulip-print tablecloths impart a garden atmosphere to the room.

WORTH AVENUE VILLA

*W*orth Avenue, one of the world's most famous shopping streets, is small compared to Manhattan's Madison Avenue or the Avenue Faubourg Saint–Honoré in Paris. Still, if Palm Beach flew a flag, its em-  blem could be interlocking Cs standing not only for clean, civil, and capricious but equally appro- priately for Cartier, Chanel, and Calvin Klein—all Worth Avenue merchants. The street is the source of legendary mercantile traditions. In the 1930s Cartier and Van Cleef & Arpels loaned tiaras as though they were operating a library. Until recently names were as good as credit cards, and women such as Jackie Onassis and Estée Lauder could buy closetsful of dresses at Saks, Martha's, and Sara Fredericks without even signing a sales slip. Typically, a purchase would be delivered to the customer's home before she returned from her lunch date and the bill would be dispatched directly to her private accountant. Rose Kennedy often ended her shopping trips to Worth Avenue simply by waiting on the corner for someone to offer her a ride home.

In the 1920s Worth Avenue had residences on its east end and a smattering of shops in arcades designed by Addison Mizner to the west. In *Palm Beach Revisited*, Judge James R. Knott's lively account of Palm Beach history, Ada Louise Huxtable, a former architecture critic for the *New York Times*, is quoted as praising Mizner's shopping arcades for their "dramatic inventiveness... a superb act of theater and urban design."

One of Palm Beach's most historic and prized residences still exists above one of these arcades. Nestled in the Via Parigi is Mimi and Russell Duncan's Worth Avenue villa, a residential tower with Robert Scott Stilin's decorating shop on the ground floor. The residence is an indirect result of Mizner's premier Palm Beach project, a private club commissioned by his friend and backer, Paris Singer (of the sewing machine fortune), who first lured the architect to Palm Beach. The first building that Singer commissioned Mizner to design was intended to be a hospital where World War I soldiers could recover from shell shock. By the time it was built, however, the war had ended and it became a private club that still exists today. Singer donated the medical equipment to the then new Delphine Dodge Hospital.

The club opened on Saturday, January 25, 1919, with twenty-five charter members. Mizner's and Singer's first joint effort was a great success. Its Moorish towers and fantastic courtyards appealed to the club's members and guests, many of whom begged Mizner to build similar residential structures. His first

Above: Sun pours into the top floor of this villa, enhancing the bright shades of the yellow living room, orange dining room, and green sun porch.

Preceding pages
Left: Via Parigi.
Right: Only steps off Worth Avenue is the Duncans' Italianate villa, built for Paris Singer by Addison Mizner. The entrance hall is decorated with four Viennese hand-painted panels. In the elevator are three murals on silk by a Milanese artist.

Right: The living room, decorated with ancestral furniture, sits high above the fashionable shops of Worth Avenue. "It's like living over a candy store," says Mimi Duncan. Through the arched windows to the east the Duncans see red tile rooftops—a Mizner trademark—and the Atlantic Ocean.

commission was from Philadelphia socialite Eva Stotesbury, often called by the social press—and by Mizner—Queen Eva.

Meanwhile, Singer continued adding on to the club almost every year, retaining Mizner as house architect. Singer requested an arcade of shops just east of the club. Eventually Mizner built his own shops across the street, where he planned to sell furniture designed for his projects. Above this arcade Mizner built a residence and office for himself, a five-story villa where Palm Beachers Terry and Mary Mahoney now live. When Singer saw it he insisted on a similar arrangement. Mizner agreed and built an adjoining arcade of shops and a six-story villa. In honor of Paris Singer, he named the complex Via Parigi (*Parigi* is "Paris" in Italian).

In the mid-1920s, shortly after the Via Parigi villa was built, Singer and Mizner began suffering serious losses—Mizner in a project to develop Boca Raton, an area about an hour south of Palm Beach, and Singer in an effort to develop a peninsula north of Palm Beach, which is still called Singer Island. Legend has it that Hugh Dillman, a former president of Singer's club, was given the opportunity to buy the Via Parigi villa as a token of appreciation for saving the club from bankruptcy in 1932.

When the Duncans heard that the historic villa was for sale some twenty years ago, they immediately flew down from Manhattan for a look. They realized that nothing could equal the villa's superb views on all sides. The northern view is of multileveled barrel-tile roofs in various shades of mismatched reds. The eastern view is of the Atlantic Ocean. To the south, the Duncans can see clear across an expansive golf course all the way to the Intracoastal Waterway and beyond to West Palm Beach's

Left: An heirloom daybed
graces this paneled sitting
room, which is part of a
guest suite.
Above: Looking south from
the arched windows of the
sun room on the top floor,
one has a sweeping view of
Worth Avenue and Palm
Beach's southern estate
section. The red barrel-tile
roof of the club that was the
very first of Addison Mizner's
many Palm Beach designs
dominates the horizon.

One of the guest suites consists of two bedrooms joined by an arched doorway. In each of the rooms is one of a pair of fine and rare eighteenth-century American canopy beds that belonged to Mimi Duncan's family in Memphis, Tennessee.

growing skyline. Unable to resist the villa, they moved out of their Manhattan town house on Riverview Terrace—just east of Sutton Place—lock, stock, and antique silver collection.

Mimi Duncan describes her interiors as "decayed gentility." All six floors are decorated with canopied beds, chests, and chairs from her family estate in Memphis, Tennessee. Her maternal grandfather, C.P.J. Mooney, was the famous Pulitzer Prize–winning publisher and editor of Memphis's *Commercial Appeal*. Her paternal grandfather was Civil War colonel Robert Galloway, who donated spacious parks to Memphis. Mimi's father was

An elegantly curved staircase joins the master bedroom suite and the top floor, where the living room, dining room, and kitchen are located, making these two floors self-contained.

administrator of the Marshall Plan in Trieste, Italy, and held the rank of ambassador.

The top floor, where the Duncans entertain, consists of a living room, dining room, sun porch, and kitchen. Below is the master bedroom, a dressing room, a sitting room, and a guest bedroom. On the fourth and third floors there are more bedrooms; the second floor is her husband's office. Here Russell Duncan, formerly chairman of the board of two New York Stock Exchange companies, continues to work as a private investor in industrial companies. The first floor is divided between the Duncans' formal entrance gallery and the decorating shop.

Mimi Duncan points out that with all these many levels she really needs only one, the top floor with its view. Despite the villa's considerable size and the fact that its tower has been struck by lightning three times, it would never occur to the Duncans to move. "We love Palm Beach and our Mizner tower," she says.

The fifth-floor guest room is painted a soothing blue, as is the rest of the floor. The portrait to the right is believed to be of Isabella Stewart Gardner.

LUXURY AFLOAT

*T*his boat was not designed to sit and drink gin off," barks *Crili* Captain David Huffman. In fact, the first improvement the new owner, a member of one  of Palm Beach's great sporting families, made after purchasing the sparkling ninety-five- foot yacht was to beef up her ability to travel extreme distances, usu- ally in hot pursuit of bluefin tuna. "Fishing for tuna is his real love," says Captain Huffman of the *Crili*'s owner. Trophies won in fishing tournaments, including the prized title of overall winner of the Cat Cay Tuna Tournament in 1984, line the walls of his office. The biggest tuna ever caught on the *Crili* was a 600-pounder landed by the owner's nephew. Indeed, the boat, so luxurious looking, is highly functional. "She was really redesigned as a water-sport base," Huffman says. State-of-the-art navigation equipment, a satellite communications

Preceding pages
Left: A life preserver bears the boat's name in typical yachting fashion.
Right: The *Crili* is the flagship of a fleet consisting of a forty-seven-foot Monterey sport fisher, a twenty-one-foot Mako boat, a bonefishing skiff, and a Yamaha Wave Runner.

Left: The floor of the heavily trafficked aft deck is carpeted with a durable synthetic sisal rug. Bielecky rattan furniture is covered in a sturdy beach print from Sunbrella Fabrics. Decorative pillows are perfect for an al fresco snooze. Lunch and dinner are served on the small table.
Right: Family snapshots depict fishing and diving trips aboard the *Crili*.

system, two 650-horsepower engines, and an oversized electrical generator were added, enabling the yacht to sail over 4,000 miles without stopping for fuel or provisions. When traveling, most often to the Bahamas or Mexico's Yucatan Peninsula, she is the hard-working mother ship of a sporting fleet and can accommodate six crew members and six guests. Usually, most of the passengers are family, including the owners' two daughters, Crista and Lillian, for whom the boat was named.

The *Crili* is also equipped with a hundred-bottle wine cellar, a cook when under way, and a massive air conditioner. "The owners aren't camping when they're not out fishing," the captain admits proudly. The owner's younger daughter, Palm Beach interior designer Lillian Fernandez, was the natural choice as decorator. Fernandez won her sea legs at a young age as her father's most faithful fishing and diving companion, and in the process she acquired a sixth sense about the proper use of space on a boat. Although she is used to working on the spacious rooms of houses in Palm Beach and South America, she understood that on this boat, everything had to serve three purposes simultaneously: beauty, function, and enough versatility to accommodate an entire family in only two public rooms.

Fernandez managed to arrange these two principal living spaces, the aft deck and the living room, so that they could hold up to twelve people comfortably for a week at a time. Fernandez took many of her design cues from the owner's onshore residence, although she used subtler colors and fabrics. "I didn't want it to be classic boat fare. We all have to live on this, so I wanted it to look more like a house," Fernandez says.

The *Crili*'s salon is furnished with an overstuffed sofa, four sandy-colored club chairs, and two rattan chairs that can be placed around a table or pulled up to a nearby bar. An ottoman serves both as a coffee table and as additional sitting space when everyone is forced inside because of inclement weather. On such occasions a game table, usually used for cards and puzzles, can also be used for dining, as can the bar.

When the weather is cooperative, the family gathers on the aft deck, which is comfortable but truly durable, as this is where everyone piles on and off the vessel when the smaller boats in the fleet tie up. In the deck's sitting area there are two rattan sofas covered with pale yellow fabric and accessorized with fish pillows. Rattan chairs can be grouped in the sitting area or pulled up to a small, expandable round table at the far end of the deck, where meals are constantly being served. Special attention is paid to the selection of colorful, oversized bath towels, fanciful straw hats, and even neon snorkeling equipment, all of which contribute to the decorating effort on this deck. Below there are two small bedrooms, as well as the master suite, which has two bathrooms and a sitting area.

"He was a tough client, but he always paid his bills," says Fernandez, who opted not to tell the sportsman that the nautical-design fabric in the master bedroom was found in a children's shop in London. Her father is learning that function and beauty, even at sea, need not be mutually exclusive.

Lillian Fernandez created sitting areas in the living room that are as practical as they are inviting. The room is decorated in shades of peach and green. To **insulate against noise, there is a specially designed Stark carpet backed by lead and foam pads. Walls and ceiling are covered with a beige fabric from Hinson & Co.**

Above: The fabric-covered walls in this cabin mute noise from the engine room. Left: "In a boat, everything is about storage," says Lillian Fernandez. She designed the beds in this cabin to accommodate everything from bottled water and towels to diving equipment. The bedspread, walls, and ceiling are covered in a blue and white nautical stripe from Hinson & Co.

BUOYANT BEACH HOUSE

After Diane de la Bégassière purchased a tiny house for a mountain of money she sat on the front steps and cried. Her tears were prompted by both joy and regret. Diane had fallen in love with Palm Beach while visiting friends in 1984 and shortly thereafter rented a place in town. She spent the next three years house hunting in Palm Beach. "The houses kept getting smaller and the prices kept getting higher," Diane recalls. Nevertheless, she continued the search and finally settled on a small north–end house that projected a certain appeal even though it did not have one architectural element in common with the design in her head. Almost reluctantly, Diane telephoned designer Sims Murray. "I didn't want to spend a lot of money but I called him to see what we could do."

GRAND COMFORT

In the 1920s, if a man could dance the tango, keep track of his playing cards, play a respectable game of golf, and trace his ancestry back to the time of Leonardo da Vinci, he could lead the good life in Palm Beach. Maurice Fatio satisfied all these requirements and more. He held a degree from Zurich's Polytechnic School of Architecture and he had earned a strong professional reputation for completing projects in Manhattan. So it should come as no surprise that Fatio became one of Palm Beach's most sought-after architects, even in an era when many of the world's renowned architects were finding it impossible to snare commissions there. Fatio opened a Palm Beach office in 1925 and, following the pattern of his New York office, was immediately engulfed with work. At the time, Addison Mizner was already established as Palm Beach's architect of choice,

**Preceding pages
Left: These Portuguese
tiles, imbedded in a wall of
the family room, are
believed to have been split
in half purposely in order to
avoid the import tax when
they were brought into the
United States in the early
1920s. Right: Fatio almost
always created ornate
entrances, as these
elaborately carved front
doors attest.**

**Left: The dramatic vaulted
ceiling in the living room is
a typical feature of Fatio's
designs. The house's
original chandelier hangs
from the hand-detailed
pecky cypress ceiling.
Against the far wall is an
1829 English breakfront.
Both sofas are upholstered
in Scalamandré silk. A
Brunschwig & Fils flame-
pattern fabric is used on
the French *berger* chair in
the foreground and a
Clarence House floral
pattern covers the
armchair. Right: The facade
of this Mediterranean-style
house is grand yet
understated.**

but Palm Beachers were tiring of Mizner's ecclesiastical touches. They preferred Fatio to Mizner because Fatio was not married to the Mediterranean style, and when he did execute it, he was inclined to hold down the holy adornments that Mizner liked to litter around his clients' estates. Just as Mizner's wealthy clients made it possible for him to import European embellishments, even during the Great Depression, Fatio's clients guaranteed his company's immunity from the Florida land bust of the early 1930s, as their fortunes

were unaffected by the caprices of the economy. Indeed, Fatio's Palm Beach client list sounds like a who's who in American enterprise, including William J. McAneen, president of Detroit Hudson Motor Company; John S. Pillsbury, of Pillsbury Flour; and Huntington Hartford of the A&P fortune. One of the houses Fatio built was labeled the "ham and cheese house" by local wits; constructed of pale coquina stone separated by strips of red brick, it did indeed bear some resemblance to a sandwich. Financier Mortimer L. Schiff, a senior member of Kuhn, Loeb & Company, commissioned it. Fatio also designed a house for Otto Kahn, another financier associated with Kuhn, Loeb. Kahn had the perfect live-in companion for a house of this magnitude. She was Rose Cumming, an eccentric but gifted decorator, known for her flamingo-red hair and cabbage-rose prints.

Many of the houses Fatio built became as renowned for their interiors as they were for their exteriors. Chicago industrialist

A statue of Poseidon,
framed by planted urns,
reigns over the
deep, blue-tiled pool.

**Right: In this small loggia
on the northern side of the
house breakfast is served at
the round glass table, while
a cozy sitting area is used
for afternoon teas.**

Patrick Lannon bought a house on South Ocean Drive that Fatio had originally designed for E. F. Hutton. Lannon had a substantial collection of modern art, and when he ran out of wall space he hung Mondrians on the ceiling. One room was devoted to primitive sculpture. Here he often set up runways to host fashion shows for designer Mary McFadden, who recruited many of her Palm Beach pals as models.

Now the house belongs to the owners of a New York hockey team, who hired British decorator Georgina Fairholmes to return it to its original grandeur with masses of English antiques and cozy chintzes, and it is again one of Palm Beach's most celebrated houses, if in a different vein.

One of Fatio's houses that no longer exists confirmed America's flowering romance with French decorative art and furniture during the 1940s. Charles Wrightsman, an oil and natural gas magnate, bought the house in 1947. His new wife, Jayne, set about decorating it in a way that established her good taste and her knowledge of fine arts and furniture. Jayne, then still new on the social scene and not quite as self-assured as she is now, observed the stylish women of Palm Beach for cues. If you weren't born with money, one sure way of establishing yourself was to collect a certain category of art and become curator of your own private museum. It was, and still is, the mansion industry of the twentieth century.

Jessie Woolworth Donahue, Martha Baird Rockefeller, and Chrysler heiress Thelma Foy were among the style setters of the 1940s. They were discovering and rapidly acquiring ornate French furniture, moving away from what they considered the puritan English look, until then a "must" in America's wealthiest

homes. In things that mattered to her Jayne was not easily outdone, and her original collection of Meissen porcelain birds grew into one of the world's most valuable collections of French decorative art and furniture. By 1959 the Wrightsmans' collection had become so large that they hired Englishman Francis Watson, a curator of Queen Elizabeth's art works and a director of the Wallace Museum, to catalog the hundreds of rare pieces. Many of the pieces that were once in the Fatio-designed house can now be seen in the Wrightsman Galleries at the Metropolitan Museum of Art in New York. Among the more notable possessions were a writing table designed in the 1740s by Bernard II Van Ryssen Burg, Louis XV gilded wood stools, a 1680 Savonnerie rug, and a red lacquer writing desk made for Louis XV by Gilles Joubert, the king's cabinetmaker, for which the Wrightsmans paid $350,000.

At the time, Jayne's love of French furniture spread like the flu through America's wealthiest circles. Social chronicler Eugenia Shepard coined the term *FFF*, for Fancy French Furniture, to imply that one's house was well appointed.

The Wrightsmans left the house in 1984, auctioning its contents through Sotheby's. The sale brought $4,800,000 for 247 pieces. The following year the house was sold for $10,000,000 to Leslie Wexner of the Limited clothing-store chain, who tore it down to build a replica of Versailles's Petit Trianon. Before the project was finished, however, he sold the plans and the property to Mediplex magnate Abe Gossman, who spent $25,000,000 to acquire the land and the plans, which were revised to his liking.

Once Fatio's architectural masterpiece was demolished, some of his other work moved up on the Palm Beach real estate list. One

Left: The loggia is furnished with oversized iron chaises longues, chairs, and antique wicker. The owners chose a pale peach and gray fabric by Rose Cummings to cover the cushions. The ceiling fans were designed for the house when it was built.

Below: This grand dining room, used only for formal occasions, is located at the southern end of the loggia.

of these, located on the south end of the island, is a prime example of Fatio's ability to design a grand-sized Mediterranean house, devoid of theatrics yet still incorporating vaulted ceilings, Moorish grillwork, barrel-tile roofs, extensive paneling, and large entertaining areas and courtyards. The owners bought it when they decided to move from Memphis to Palm Beach, giving up a winter house in Hobe Sound, Florida. After looking at dozens of properties they settled on this one because its generous rooms were so well suited to the husband's six-foot-plus height.

When they acquired the house it was icy white from walls to draperies. "The painting didn't enhance the beautiful vaulted ceilings and arches," says the wife. She knew she wanted soothing tones and insisted on something different from the bright colors expected in a subtropical setting, so in collaboration with painter Frank Maino she created a type of "greige," a combination of gray and beige.

Once the background was established, she began to make the place cozy. "We're Southern and our houses have always been comfortable and warm," she says. The couple has lived in Moscow, Geneva, Memphis, and the English countryside, and has tailored each residence to suit its surroundings and their style. The wife

had definite ideas about what would be appropriate in Florida. "I didn't use the faded fabrics I used in Memphis, but everything in Florida doesn't have to be pink and green," she says. "You really have to look at fabric in the light; the light here is so different from the light in Memphis, which is different from the light in England."

A self-proclaimed Anglophile, she has a tendency to create an intimate, cluttered look. An abundance of landscape paintings and family photographs emphasizes the warm yet rich feeling of Fatio's design. The house also reveals another of Fatio's talents. His architecture is not rigidly nationalistic. Successive owners can change the flag by changing the furniture without erasing Fatio's signature.

One unabashedly imposing piece that the owners insist on installing in every house and that is often the starting point of their decorating efforts is a grand piano. "Ninety-eight percent of the time we end up around the piano singing at the end of a party," says the wife, a highly accomplished singer who gives concerts throughout the United States and Europe. Guests join in, flat or in perfect pitch, responding not only to the urging of the host, but also to the warmth of the surroundings.

Left: The courtyard is decorated with a fountain designed by Fatio. Countless palm trees keep the area cool and provide a reprieve from the sun.

BERMUDA-STYLE BEACHFRONT

The residents of the Lake Worth Cottage Colony, as Palm Beach was called before 1878, formed the island's version of the Mayflower Society. Originally, there were about nineteen families living in modest clapboard structures along the eastern banks of Lake Worth. The properties of the early families often extended all the way across the narrow island to the ocean. But these prudent colonists avoided building on the ocean side  where hurricane winds and salt spray made maintenance of wooden dwellings a never-ending responsibility. This preference for living on the lake was passed on to second- and third-generation Palm Beachers. But the most valuable properties of all were those that had their own inland lakes because they were secluded and protected from the elements. One of these prized lakes stretched between the street Miraflores to the south and the Palm Beach Country Club to the north, and extended 500 feet east and west as part of the Henry, Cluett,

Maddock, and Merrill estates. This group of families treasured their inland lake, which by World War II was a rarity. In 1941, however, the town and county governments ordered the privately owned lake to be filled in because another access road to the north end of the island was needed. The road was called North Lake Trail, the name it still bears.

All the owners, except for Charles Merrill, reluctantly filled in their portion of the lake. Merrill cleverly built a dike to keep his part intact. His estate, Merrill's Landing, was located just south of what is now Plantation Road and just north of the historic house Duck's Nest. Merrill's daughter, Doris Magowan, remembers approaching her father's house across a little bridge over the lake, which was surrounded by fuzzy Australian pines. This unique variety of pine, which now fills in the entire area, usually grows where there was once a lake or a swamp.

Charles Merrill, a founder of the Merrill Lynch brokerage house, bought Merrill's Landing from the Cluett family and hired architect Howard Major to design a house and other buildings to give the estate the effect of a plantation. When Major arrived in Palm Beach in 1925, he was taken aback by the prevalence of what he considered bastardized Spanish, Moorish, and Mediterranean architecture. He proceeded to carve an architectural niche for himself in the town, designing Georgian-style houses modified for the subtropical climate, often taking his cues from the Bahamas, Jamaica, and Bermuda. A small cluster of buildings called Major Alley, built in the mid-1920s, remains the most visible testimony to his advocation of Georgian architecture. For Merrill, Major designed a Southern-style plantation house complete with a huge porch, reminiscent of

Preceding pages
Left: At Mrs. Magowan's suggestion, architect Howard Major designed this Bermuda-style house with its gabled roofs, cheerful pink exterior, and crisp white woodwork in 1958.
Right: Mrs. Magowan enjoys painting on the balcony overlooking the pool.

Above: The dining room table is set with Tiffany flatware, Audubon plates, and small glass decanters. The Venetian wine goblets are from the Jack Davidson boutique in Palm Beach. The lilies came from Doris Magowan's garden.

Right: The dining room, which was added to the original plans, accommodates two tables. "I got the cart before the horse," says Doris Magowan, who designed the house around the land and the furniture.

Wildwood, the Merrills' Greenville, Mississippi, plantation. A miniature Jeffersonian promenade led to the property's guest house and an outbuilding used by Mickey, the family's boat captain and handyman. There was also a small guest house and a house for the help.

The main house stood on the lake side of the ocean-to-lake estate, but the family often barbecued on the ocean side, thrashing their way through thick sea oats to get there. The ocean property was bequeathed to Doris in 1956. The lakeside portion of the sixteen acres was sold by Mr. Merrill's estate for the benefit of the newly created Charles E. Merrill Trust. Mrs. Magowan decided to build on the lush oceanfront footage she remembered so fondly, as by then cement construction made houses resistant to the sea's salty winds.

She had been keeping a notebook of the components she wanted to include in a residence. Like her father, she turned her list over to architect Howard Major. "I asked him to incorporate certain things into the house," she says. First, a winding driveway leading from the public access road to the house; second, a beautifully landscaped lawn stretching from the house to the ocean. But because the public access road ran near the ocean, with Magowan's property in between, it would have been impossible to fulfill both wishes. Magowan ended up with a pastoral landscape that from the beach looks like one of the best maintained fairways in America. As an imaginative alternative to a winding driveway from the road, a single, strategically placed curve affords the house complete privacy.

Magowan also suggested building the house in Bermuda style because she felt that the gabled roof lines and sunny open spaces

With its bright upholstery, sisal rug, and colorful pillows, the library is a book lover's delight. The master bedroom, which overlooks the ocean, can be seen through the doorway.

of this style were right for subtropical living. She told Major what pieces of furniture she wanted to use. Together, architect and visionary worked on the plans, frequently consulting each other by phone, Major from Florida and Magowan from San Francisco, New York City, or Long Island.

The long-distance collaboration resulted in one of Palm Beach's most charming residences. Its upbeat pink facade is accentuated by crisp white overhangs and shutters at every window. Inside it is the airy, manageable space Magowan had envisioned.

Four discrete sitting areas make up the spacious living room. The library is seriously bookish, its shelves filled with cherished volumes, but it is far from dreary. A sisal rug, and sofas and club chairs covered in a beige fabric with bright red and yellow flowers, suit its sunny setting.

Over the years a series of small buildings that conform to the style and setting of the original Bermuda house have been added. First a little cottage for the help, now blanketed with climbing roses, was built to the northwest of the house. Next a garage with guest quarters over it was added to the southwest. The guest quarters' little balcony overlooks the final addition, a pool with a circular, peaked-roof gazebo, built in 1986, many years after the original house was completed.

Despite these additions, Magowan's house remains low-key and unpretentious, its style firmly rooted in the traditions of turn-of-the-century Palm Beachers, who knew how to achieve authentic island appeal.

The pool is situated in front of the house to protect it from strong ocean winds. A Bermuda–style cabana was built at the northern end. To the left is Mrs. Magowan's herb and flower garden.

CONTEMPORARY DRAMA

*A*rt dealer Arij Gasiunasen is a matchmaker; it is his job to introduce artists to collectors. And his house is an indispensable part of his business, a place where he can show clients and friends—often the same people  —how dramatic works by such artists as Karel Appel, Jim Dine, and Alex Katz can be as effective in a private environment as they are in galleries and museums. Gasiunasen had no intention of establishing his business in Palm Beach until he ran into Toronto friends Catherine and Stephanie Hill on a flight from Paris to Toronto. The Hills, a mother and daughter who operate one of Toronto's most exclusive fashion boutiques, were contemplating closing their Palm Beach store. They offered to lease the highly visible space on the corner of Worth Avenue and South County Road to Gasiunasen. He was intrigued and challenged by the idea, so before the plane landed, the deal was made.

Setting up shop on Worth Avenue was one thing, finding a house to showcase his private collection and accommodate his penchant for entertaining was quite another. Gasiunasen, who had resided in everything from a sprawling apartment with loftlike living areas to a cozy house with small rooms, was not sure what he was looking for, but he was confident he would know the right house when he saw it. He finally decided on a house on Seaview Avenue within walking distance of his gallery.

The location has an appealing history. Seaview Avenue was part of the first major Palm Beach development since Henry Morrison Flagler had begun building in the late 1800s. The Palm Beach Improvement Company decided to develop all the land between the ocean and the Intracoastal Waterway, bordered on the north by Seaview Avenue and on the south by what is now Worth Avenue. In 1901 a sea wall was built on the lake side and a hydraulic dredge was used to fill in the lagoons that dotted the grassy marshlands. It took two hundred men working day and night for months to complete the project by 1910. An avenue running through the middle of the development was designed to replicate Chicago's broad, elegant Drexel Boulevard. It was named, and is still called, Royal Palm Way.

In 1913 the Royal Park Bridge connecting the barrier island of Palm Beach and West Palm Beach on the mainland was built at the end of Royal Palm Way. The rickety wooden structure was financially supported by tolls until 1918 when the county took it over and replaced it with a masonry bridge. The replacement bridge collapsed in 1921, just as the builders were putting on the finishing touches. Another replacement was finally ready in 1924. It, too, was faulty; its drawbridge constantly jammed. Finally, in

Preceding pages
Left: The entrance hall serves as a gallery. In the foreground is Lynn Chadwick's bronze *Second Girl Sitting on a Bench*. An untitled Bruce McLean painting (1982) hangs on the wall to the right and at the end of the hall is a charcoal and graphite work by Robert Longo. Right: In front of the house are two casts of Jim Dine's bronze *The Columbia River* (1988).

Left: Kenneth Noland's painting *Anew* (1967) hangs over a Biedermeier table-and-chairs ensemble in a corner of the living room.
Right: Two paintings, Alex Katz's *The Dance* (1978) and Karel Appel's *Flying Faces* (1961), dominate the living room, with its Russian Biedermeier tub chairs, faux Biedermeier piano, and coffee table by Arman.

The library is painted deep red to set off an untitled work by Arman that is executed in acrylic paint and paint tubes. Lynn Chadwick's *Winged Figures IV* sits on the round table to the left.

The dramatic dining room with its purple walls and recessed mirrors opens onto a small patio. Karel Appel's *Lover's II* hangs on the wall.

1959, a wide, four-lane bridge was built to last. Still in operation, it is one of the three main links between Palm Beach and the mainland. Locally it is called the middle bridge because it is located between the Southern Boulevard crossing to the south and the Flagler Bridge just a mile to the north.

There were many things about Gasiunasen's new house that were not to his taste, including a burnt orange door and a drab white interior. What did appeal to Gasiunasen was more permanent. "If you like the bones of a house, buy it," he says, so buy it he did, both for its floor plan, which reminded him of a rambling apartment, and for its generous hedges, which transform the terraces off most of the rooms into private enclaves.

In Toronto, Gasiunasen had worked with the late interior designer Leo Scarth La Ferme, who knew the dealer's tendency toward the unusual. Gasiunasen brought many of the pieces La

Right: "Revolution" (1971), a darkly humorous gouache by Alexander Calder, hangs in the bedroom.
Facing page:
Zebra prints add an exotic touch to the master bedroom. Eric Fischl's "Study for Black Sea" (1986) hangs over the bed.

Ferme had chosen with him to Palm Beach. "I like to calculate my environment," says Gasiunasen, who hired Palm Beach designer Scott Snyder to arrange the decor so that it would dramatize his art collection. "Most galleries are icy white. We used warm colors one wouldn't normally see in a gallery space so people could realize that even large-scale art can create a warm setting," Snyder says. One work by Alex Katz was so large that an entire picture window in the living room was sealed up to create wall space for it.

The living room is painted a deep beige and the furniture is Biedermeier, the mid-nineteenth-century German style that simplified the opulently neoclassic elements of French Empire, clearing the way for Art Nouveau and Art Deco. Gasiunasen even had his white Baldwin baby grand restyled to resemble his Biedermeier pieces after three dealers searched in vain on three continents for a genuine Biedermeier piano. The lines of the Biedermeier furniture are clean enough for attention to be focused on massive canvases by Alex Katz, Milton Avery, and Karel Appel. There are two lighting circuits in the living room. One board has "normal" lighting; the other controls the halogen quartz lights that illuminate the paintings. When entertaining, Gasuinasen romanticizes the lighting effects with candles. For large parties Scott Snyder designs table settings and centerpieces.

In the dining room, deep purple walls emphasize the rich violets in Karel Appel's painting *Lovers II*. Mirrors set inside semicircular encasements reflect huge vases filled with hydrangeas, creating a magic environment. Thus the fantasy and emotionalism of modern art, which are often difficult to convey to potential buyers, can effectively speak for themselves.

PALM BEACH ROCOCO

Marjorie Merriweather Post, the only child of cereal tycoon C.W. Post, always knew what she wanted. In Palm Beach during the 1920s, such certitude was hardly a distinguishing characteristic, but Mrs. Post also knew how to get what she wanted, so when she decided to build Mar-a-Lago (which means "from the ocean to the lake"), a palatial winter house that would dramatize her position in society and set her above the loftiest doyennes in town, she hired Joseph Urban, a master at creating dramatic illusions. A Viennese, Urban had designed many well-known buildings in Europe for clients such as the khedive of Egypt and Emperor Franz Joseph of Austria before coming to New York in 1914. Marjorie Post inherited her father's business—founded in 1895 on the production of the coffee substitute

The fanciful chimneys Joseph Urban created, seen here from the lookout tower, lend Mar-a-Lago the feel of a fairy-tale castle.

Postum and the breakfast cereal Post Toasties—plus a vast family fortune when she was only twenty-seven years old. She began using her wealth at full throttle, not only spending lavishly on herself and on charitable causes, but astutely managing her investments.

She enlarged the fortune greatly, creating General Foods, the umbrella company that marketed the many food lines she added to Post cereals. It was Marjorie who insisted that the company buy Birds-Eye frozen foods, for example. The deal came about during her marriage to Edward F. Hutton. Once, while they were sailing on their yacht, *Sea Cloud*, the chef happened to serve goose and, impressed by its taste, Marjorie asked him how he managed to serve game at sea. He informed her that it came from a man who had developed a food-freezing process in Gloucester, Massachusetts. Marjorie realized the mass-market appeal of the process but her husband and Post Company executives advised the heiress against buying it for a nominal fee compared to the $22 million they paid for it four years later, in 1929, at Marjorie's wise insistence.

Marjorie married Edward F. Hutton in 1920 and they became an international society sensation. They had valid credentials, including the 317-foot *Sea Cloud*, which had a working fireplace and state rooms furnished with antiques; a Manhattan mansion on the corner of 92nd Street and Fifth Avenue, acquired from the Burden family; a country place in Roslyn, Long Island; a plantation and shooting preserve in South Carolina; Topnotch, a retreat in the Adirondacks; and a British Viscount airplane powered by four Rolls Royce engines, with a crew of five. The large passenger plane shuttled royals, notables in the military and

Preceding pages Left: On Mar-a-Lago's sweeping back lawn is the pool that was added by Donald Trump. The steps on either side of the fountain lead to the mansion's theatrical courtyard. To the right of the pool is the bathroom, which was designed by Marion Sims Wyeth in the 1960s. Right: These figures in the portico are examples of Viennese sculptor Franz Barwig's elaborate stonework.

Right: The decor of the living room, which the current owner, Donald Trump, has not changed, was inspired by the seven rare silk Italian needle-point panels that grace the walls. The gilded ceiling was modeled after the Thousand-Wing ceiling of Venice's Accademia.

This portico on Mar–a–Lago's northern side created a dramatic prelude to the elaborate parties Mrs. Post hosted.

diplomatic worlds, and members of the glittering international society set back and forth to Mar-a-Lago.

At the time, prominent social columnist Maury Paul published a list of fifty families whom he dubbed "Old Guard Society," including the Vanderbilts, the Goelets, and the Van Rensselaers, to which he added fifty new names of socially established women whom he called "Cafe Society." Among them were Mrs. William Burden, Mrs. John Drexel, Mrs. Jay Gould, Mrs. Joseph Widener, Mrs. Edward Stotesbury, and, from Battle Creek, Michigan, Mrs. Edward F. Hutton. In that era Mrs. Stotesbury ("Queen Eva") was the reigning social monarch of Palm Beach. Her husband was a partner in the Morgan firm. Eva was once heard interrupting two men bragging about their financial victories: "The only astute business move I ever made was marrying Mr. Stotesbury," she said. Indeed, her marriage enabled her to commission the first Palm Beach mansion designed by Mizner. It had a forty-car garage and a private zoo next to a lakefront tea house.

Like Eva, Marjorie loved to entertain, and the fairy-tale castle Mar-a-Lago put her on the map as an international hostess. Upon seeing the finished house E. F. Hutton was said to have cried, "I wanted a beach house and look at what I got." The house was so awe-inspiring that it was the first structure in the Palm Beach area to be documented and recorded in the archives of the Historic American Building Survey and the Library of Congress.

Mar-a-Lago was originally designed by Marion Sims Wyeth, a well-respected Palm Beach architect. He began the project in 1923, and by 1925 Post had one of Palm Beach's grandest estates. But Joseph Urban took over the project after Post, who met him through friends Flo Ziegfeld, Billie Burke, and Anthony

Architect Joseph Urban designed a dramatic cloistered arcade on the lake side of Mar-a-Lago. The fifteenth-century Spanish glazed tiles that embellish the walls are part of original owner Marjorie Post's vast collection.

Biddle, gave him a tour of her new house. No sooner did Urban start suggesting ways Marjorie could revamp the brand new house than the entire project was in his hands. He spent the next two-and-a-half years redesigning and redecorating Mar-a-Lago's first floor, converting the original servants' quarters to guest suites, and adding new staff quarters. A host of artisans collaborated with Urban on Mar-a-Lago. Viennese sculptor Franz Barwig and his son came from Austria and set up a studio on the premises. They worked for nearly three years designing the mansion's elaborate stonework and woodwork. Italian and Portuguese artisans were commissioned to execute the Barwigs' and Urban's designs. The ironwork was cast and wrought in West Palm Beach. Florida cypress was used for the doors and beams, and the roof was covered in Cuban barrel tiles. Three shiploads of Dorian stone, in which tiny seashells and fossils can be seen, were brought from Genoa, Italy, for the exterior walls and arches. Among the decorative features are 36,000 antique Spanish tiles, many dating back to the fifteenth century.

The dining room is a copy of a room in Rome's Chigi Palace. The library is paneled in old English walnut and the living room's gold-leaf ceiling is a copy of the Thousand-Wing ceiling in Venice's Accademia. The guest suites are as lavish as Hollywood sets; each is designed around a different theme, including a Spanish room laden with wood carvings, an Adams room with intricate moldings and reliefs, a Dutch room with a Delft-tile fireplace, and an American room with lacy bed coverlets.

Marjorie's youngest child, Nedenia, now known as Dina Merrill, was only two years old when the house was designed, and for her Urban created an opulent Sleeping Beauty room decorated with

Left: The decor of the dining room, with its two gold chandeliers, marble columns, and murals of sea life, was inspired by a room in Rome's Chigi palace. The *pietra dura* table was custom-made in Florence and became known in Palm Beach as "the million-dollar table."

Mrs. Post, known for her lavish entertaining, invited as many as two hundred guests to her formal teas. For these events she had countless services of china and crystal, all of which remained in the house after Donald Trump purchased it.

relief flowers on the walls and a curvaceous fireplace, as well as an adjoining playroom. "He let fantasy run wild," Merrill says.

After years of building, decorating, and landscaping, the estimated $1 million cost had swelled to $8 million. The completed mansion consisted of 115 rooms; its eighteen ocean-to-lake acres included expansive gardens, a nine-hole golf course, and a tunnel leading to Mrs. Post's cabanas at a private club across the street.

"There is nothing like that house in America," says Dina Merrill, who fondly remembers growing up in it at the feet of her

Above and right: For Marjorie Merriweather Post's youngest daughter, Nedenia, more familiarly known as actress Dina Merrill, Urban designed nothing short of a fairy-tale princess suite known as "Deenie's house." The door handles are gilded squirrels and the custom-made carpet depicts knights, ladies, and elves. The canopied bed has finials of carved squirrels. The focal point of the bedroom is a beehive-shaped fireplace. The walls are ornamented with a plaster relief of vines, roses, and canaries.

mother's party guests. "Mother loved to entertain," she says. She recalls one dinner party that her father particularly enjoyed. "Dad had a wonderful sense of humor and he found an actor in town to pretend to be a waiter." Hutton instructed the actor to insult the guests ruthlessly and Marjorie was appalled. She insisted that the waiter be dismissed, whereupon, Dina Merrill remembers, "He got on his hands and knees in front of mother and begged not to be let go, saying he had eight children." When the truth finally came out, Marjorie didn't speak to her husband for a week.

Dinner was often held on the patio, which was decorated with multicolored stones from beaches on Long Island Sound and plantings of gumbo-limbos and fishtail palms. Lights projecting from the estate's lookout tower bathed the patio in a soft glow.

Marjorie spared no expense for dramatic effect. Once she hired the entire Ringling Bros. and Barnum & Bailey Circus from their headquarters in Venice, Florida, for a circus party. For another event she imported the whole cast and orchestra of a Broadway musical. For her frequent square dances she hired twelve professional dancers. A staff of forty changed uniforms three times a day to accommodate the hectic schedule.

Although Marjorie was a resident of Washington, D.C., she was made an honorary citizen of Florida in 1965 by an act of the Florida Legislature. She remains the only person in the history of the state to have received such an honor, which was bestowed upon her on the floor of the Florida Senate in Tallahassee. She was praised for "her immeasurable contribution to the fame and good name of the State and her interest in numerous Florida philanthropies" and for "her benefactions in education, war

The five-story tower includes this Art Deco room, which Urban designed as a lighthearted antidote to the mansion's rococo public rooms.

Left: The ornately furnished master bedroom looks much as it did when originally designed for Marjorie Merriweather Post.

Above: When Mar-a-Lago was finished in 1927, it was the most opulent house in Palm Beach. Even this dressing room in the master suite is heavily gilded, laden with marble, and appointed with French furniture.

relief, hospitals and aid to American youth, as evidenced by her receiving decorations from five foreign governments, honorary degrees from three American universities and countless citations."

Marjorie continued her humanitarian acts until her death in 1973 at age eighty-six. Mar-a-Lago was offered to the state, but the offer was not accepted because Governor Caldwell was afraid of the traffic jams tourists would cause on already slow-moving South Ocean Boulevard. Eventually it was offered to the United States Government as a place to entertain foreign diplomats, but Washington considered it too expensive to maintain and returned it to the Post Foundation.

Mar-a-Lago remained in the Post Foundation until Donald Trump purchased it in 1985. Trump first saw the house while vacationing in Palm Beach in 1982. At that time it was listed for sale at $25 million. Trump bid $15 million but his offer was immediately rejected. In 1985, after many other bids fell through, Trump bid again, this time offering only $5 million for the house and $3 million for the furniture. His offer was accepted. After the deal was closed the *Palm Beach Daily News* ran a headline: MAR-A-LAGO'S BARGAIN PRICE ROCKS COMMUNITY.

Although Trump has turned the house into a private club, he has left just about everything intact, even the placement of the furniture. Behind the house he built a tennis court and a pool, for which he imported Dorian stone and hired local artisans to match the house's original courtyard. In his book *Art of the Deal,* Trump claims that he never relaxes. But if he were to, he admits. it would be at Mar-a-Lago, which he considers as close to paradise as he will ever get.

Selected Bibliography

Amory, Cleveland.
The Last Resorts. New York:
Harper & Bros., 1952.

Aronson, Joseph.
The Encyclopedia of Furniture.
New York: Crown Publishers,
1965.

Ash, Agnes, and Bill Olendorf.
The Palm Beach Sketchbook.
Chicago: Olendorf Graphics,
1988.

Ash, Jennifer.
"Our Palm Beach Story: Some
Insights into the Pleasures of
South Florida's Toniest Resort."
Diversion, December 1990,
pp. 87–92, 152–54.

Birmingham, Stephen.
*Our Crowd: The Great Jewish
Families of New York.* New York,
Evanston, and London: Harper &
Row, 1967.

—*The Right People: A Portrait
of the American Social
Establishment.* Boston: Little
Brown & Co., 1968.

Bowles, Hamish.
"C. Z. Guest." *Harper's &
Queen,* September 1990,
pp. 220–25.

Brookes, John.
The Indoor Garden Book. New
York: Crown Publishers, 1986.

Clarke, Gerald.
Capote. New York: Simon and
Schuster, 1988.

Curl, Donald W.
*Mizner's Florida: American
Resort Architecture.* New York,
Cambridge, and London:
Architectural History Foundation
and MIT Press, 1984.

Fairbanks, Douglas, Jr.
"Famous Parsonage." *Vogue,*
January 1978, pp. 132–35.

Fleming, John; Hugh Honour;
and Nikolaus Pevsner.
3rd ed. *Dictionary of
Architecture.* London and New
York: Penguin Books, 1980.

Gilmore, Francis.
"History of Palm Beach County
Art Club: One of the Fascinating
Chapters in Annals of the City."
Palm Beach Post Times,
February 17, 1924.

Hoffstot, Barbara D.
*Landmark Architecture of Palm
Beach.* Pittsburgh: Ober Park
Associates, 1980.

James, Henry.
The American Scene. New York:
Harper & Bros., 1907.

Johnson, Shirley and
Roberto Schezen.
Palm Beach Houses. New York:
Rizzoli International
Publications, 1991.

Kahn, E. J., Jr.
*Jock: The Life and Times of John
Hay Whitney.* Garden City, N. Y.:
Doubleday & Co., 1981.

Knott, James R.
*The Mansion Builders: Palm
Beach Revisited III.* Privately
printed, 1990.

—*Palm Beach Revisited:
Historical Vignettes of Palm
Beach County.* Privately printed,
1987.

—*Palm Beach Revisited II:
Historical Vignettes of Palm
Beach.* Privately printed, 1988.

Ney, John.
*Palm Beach: The Places, the
People, the Pleasures, the
Palaces.* Boston: Little, Brown &
Co., 1966.

Nguyen, Khoi.
"Gilt Complex: The Story of
Jayne Wrightsman."
Connoisseur, September 1991,
pp. 72–81.

Pallesen, Gayle.
"Grand Estates." *Palm Beach
Life,* May 1991, pp. 30–35,
52–53.

Romoser, Chris.
"Trump Tries PUD for Estate."
Palm Beach Daily News, Sunday,
September 22, 1991, pp. 1, A11.

Sallah, Michael.
"First Historic District Is
Designated" *Palm Beach Daily
News,* February 4, 1982,
pp. 1, A5.

Sefcovic, Enid.
"Landmarks of Time." *Palm
Beach Daily News,* Sunday,
September 24, 1989, pp. B1, B7.

Spencer, Wilma Bell.
*Palm Beach: A Century of
Heritage.* Washington D.C.:
Mount Vernon Publishing Co.,
1946.

Taylor, John.
"The Palm Beach Story." *New
York Magazine,* May 20, 1991,
pp. 30–37.

Trump, Donald. and
Tony Schwartz.
Trump: The Art of the Deal. New
York: Warner Books, 1987.

Van de Water, Ava.
"The Grand Tour." *Palm Beach
Post Times,* Sunday, December
16, 1990, pp. 1F, 11F–14F.

Vitek, Jack.
"Grace Period." *Palm Beach Life,*
October 1990, pp. 41–50.